KEEPING & BREEDING
COCKATIELS
A COMPLETE GUIDE

DULCIE & FREDDIE COOKE

Photographs by Dennis Avon

BLANDFORD PRESS
London · New York · Sydney

First published in the UK 1987 by Blandford Press
Artillery House, Artillery Row, London SW1P 1RT

Text copyright ©1987 Dulcie Cooke

Distributed in the United States by
Sterling Publishing Co. Inc.
2 Park Avenue, New York, NY 10016

Distributed in Australia by
Capricorn Link (Australia) Pty Ltd
PO Box 665, Lane Cove, NSW 2066

British Library Cataloguing in Publication Data

Cooke, Dulcie
  Keeping and breeding cockatiels : a complete
  guide.
  1. Cockatiel
  I. Title   II. Cooke, Freddie
  636. 6'865   SF473. C6

ISBN 0 7137 1961 3

Typeset by Poole Typesetting (Wessex) Limited, Bournemouth
Printed in Great Britain by Biddles Ltd., Guildford & Kings Lynn

Contents

Preface

Writing a book is an act of creation, and all creation is hard work, whether it be painting a picture, inventing something, creating a garden out of a wilderness, or writing a book on cockatiels! Without the understanding and enormous written contribution of my husband Freddie, this book would have taken so long to write, the first part would have needed revising before the last part was finished. It has been a triumph of cooperation between myself and Freddie, Mr Alan Jones B.Vet. Med. MRCVS; Mr Dennis Avon MIOP ARPS, and Mr Steve Lings, Member of the Wildlife Artists' Association.

This book has been written especially for cockatiel owners and breeders all over the world, but much of its contents would apply equally to many seed-eating species of parakeets and parrots.

It could be said that it all began with a single sentence, 'For the love of birds'. My earliest memory, at the age of four, is of standing transfixed by the beauty of a pair of cochin fowl in a huge cage, proudly surveying their admirers at a village flower show. I will never know how they got there. Perhaps their owner thought their attendance might increase her chances in the section for the biggest dahlias. From the age of thirteen years, when my father, then a retired architect, built my first two aviaries, I kept at various times British and foreign finches, doves, poultry, budgerigars, canaries, foreign softbills, large and small parrots and parakeets, and even a colony of lories; these last, some of the most fascinating birds I have ever known.

My life has been very active and varied here in the UK and briefly in Sydney, Australia; and world travels have ever increased my love of and interest in birds. It has steadily grown with the years to embrace every aspect of aviculture, and the love of wild birds as well. Our birds in aviaries in the garden, birds as ceramics, in oils and water colours, on photographic slides, prints and portraits, mingle with innumerable much-valued books and magazines to form an ever increasing kaleidoscope of colour, form and memories.

Of course, the greatest love of all is our collection of living birds in their aviaries. The search is constant to improve the husbandry of Freddie's and my collection; and, through writing, to help others who have taken up this wonderful pastime. In aviculture one learns something new every day, and very often it is the newcomers, with their fresh approach to the subject, who can contribute greatly to the accumulation of collective knowledge, to which all of us endeavour to add something of value.

Dulcie Cooke

Acknowledgements

Freddie and I wish to thank Alan Jones B.Vet. Med. MRCVS for his valuable contributions on diseases, Dennis Avon MIOP ARPS for his beautiful photographic work, and Steve Lings for his artistic sketches and drawings. Our thanks go also to the breeders of cockatiels who have helped us so much with various aspects of this book. To Mr Brian Pettit and Mr Simon Joshua for their advice on genetics; to Mr Terry Cole for the information he has made available to us on the subject of the Dominant Silver Mutation; and to Mr R. Whitby for the information on his breeding of the Lutino Pearl mutation.

Our thanks also to Mr Robin Haigh for his advice on incubation, and we wish to extend our grateful thanks to the American Cockatiel Society for providing the information on their show standards.

Finally, but by no means least, we both thank Mrs Thelma Batchelor for turning our respective handwriting into an immaculately typed manuscript.

Dulcie Cooke

Illustrations
All colour photographs by Dennis Avon MIOP, ARPS; except Plates 1, 17, 33, 34 and 35 by the authors; black and white photos by the authors.

Other illustrations by: Dennis Avon (pages 39, 41, 48, 88 and 98); Steve Lings (pages 11, 12, 16, 17, 37 and 38); Anita Lawrence (page 103); Ray Hutchins (page 105).

Introduction
Nymphicus hollandicus:
The Wild Cockatiel in
Nature and Art

The wild cockatiel is widely distributed over much of Australia, sometimes in small family groups, but also in great flocks. The birds are nomadic, particularly in the northern regions, but tend to frequent areas where trees border rivers, and where they can find various grass and other seeds. They are occasionally seen in paddocks, picking up grain, and will sometimes raid crops, particularly sorghum; they also eat berries and acacia seeds. In spite of their liking for various crops, they are not classified as pests; as is unfortunately the case with some of Australia's most beautiful parrots.

The cockatiel's flight is swift and straight, showing its white wing

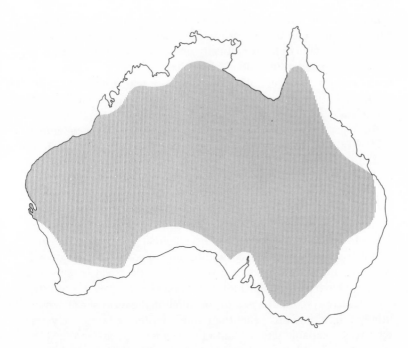

Australia, showing natural distribution of cockatiels in the wild.

patches, which gave rise to the name cockatoo parrot. The birds nest in hollows in either living or dead trees, generally eucalyptus, standing near water. Usually about five eggs are laid, but it may be more; they are deposited on decaying wood in the bottom of the hollow chosen as the nest site.

Early in the nineteenth century colonists were moving into Australia and reports and information regarding the unusual and unknown wildlife of this practically unexplored continent began to be received back in England. At that time the English ornithologist John Gould was successfully producing and selling natural history books, mainly on birds, with beautiful illustrations provided by his wife Elizabeth.

Amongst the new colonists were some relatives, who were sending back details of the beautiful and unknown birds of Australia. John Gould and his wife decided to exploit the opportunity offered to expand their work, and in 1838 visited Australia. It was their books and illustrations of birds, following their return in 1840, which brought the cockatiel to the attention of the public. The fact that the birds were so plentiful and endearing led to their great popularity.

Cockatiels have not been the subject of great paintings to the same extent as some parrots and cockatoos, and of course domestic fowl, which figure in the works of artists such as the great seventeenth century Dutch painter Melchior d'Hondecoeter. However, one artist who has left a record of a pair of cockatiels in the form of a charming lithograph, is Edward Lear, the famous writer of nonsense verse, who was a capable painter and lithographer. His life spanned the time when Gould was active with his portraits of birds, and it was

Gould who employed Edward Lear to execute some of the paintings in his books. This is recorded in Dr A.M. Lysaght's book, *The Book of Birds,* published in 1975 by Phaidon Press and as a reprint in 1984 by Chancellor Press.

Perhaps it is not too much to hope that some of the young painters of this age will turn their attention to the portrayal of these delightful birds, following the example of that outstanding photographer Dennis Avon, who provided the portraits for this book.

1 Pet Cockatiels: Their Care and Training

Of all the medium-sized and small birds which are available as pets, there is no doubt in my mind that the cockatiel is far and away the best. No other bird has such endearing ways and although others, such as some budgerigars, may be more talented talkers, few can surpass the cockatiel's ability to pour out affection to its owner.

It is very important for the would-be pet owner to avoid certain mistakes which can cause both owner and bird a lot of misery. Do *not* buy or accept as a gift an adult bird or birds which have previously lived in an aviary. They will *never* make good pets, will be frustrated and unhappy, and will very likely never become tame.

Some very young birds are also quite unsuitable pets: they were 'wild' before they got out of the nest, but will make good breeding stock for someone in later life. There are a small proportion of birds bred each year which are naturally tame and confiding and, although brought up by their parents, will come towards their owner and will even fly onto his or her head or shoulders.

A naturally confident and inquisitive cockatiel will settle in a cage very quickly, especially if it is placed where it can see and hear what is happening in the home. Every cockatiel, as with any other bird, is an individual and, if possible, the pet should be matched to the future owner. A potentially very tame but nervous bird should not be given or sold as a pet for children or young people, it would be better as a pet for an elderly person, who will be likely to understand its anxiety better. Hens are best not supplied to people who want a future talker, or one that whistles; cocks are very much more likely to learn to speak and to whistle tunes. They also often develop a most attractive song. Some elderly people enjoy the more gentle and very affectionate nature of hen cockatiels.

People buying or receiving a pet bird for the first time should seek advice on the type of cage most suitable for a cockatiel; I would suggest the bigger the better. The actual measurements should be not less than 10 in (25.4cm) wide by 15 in (38.1cm) long by 18 in (45.72cm) high; with good sized clip-on food and water containers. Very young birds are usually happiest with small food and water containers on the floor of the cage. Paper is a good floor covering for birds up to the age of about three months, with plenty of seed and grit scattered on the floor; this way they eat much more, which is very good for them. The paper and seed, etc., should be fresh daily.

Every breeder of cockatiels knows what to tell prospective owners

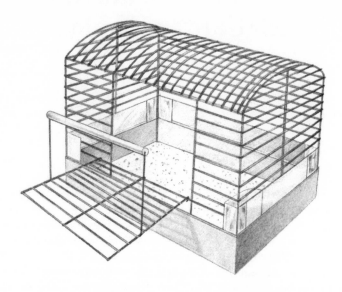

of a cockatiel, and how to feed their pet adequately, but not all assistants in pet shops make sure the buyer understands how to look after the pet they are buying. The prospective owner must make sure that he or she buys the largest and nicest cage that can be afforded. Cockatiels need plenty of space because they stand rather upright and have a broad wingspan. Even a young one cannot get its head into canary-sized food and water containers. Many nice cages now have plastic perches, but too many, too large, or sometimes too small in diameter for the comfort of a cockatiel. Two wood doweling perches ½ in (1.27cm) in diameter, are sufficient and comfortable for the bird.

A pet cockatiel needs almost exactly the same feeding as one destined for breeding. A good basic food for a daily diet is one part canary seed, one part mixed millets and one part mixed sunflower seeds. Brown bread soaked first in water then milk, squeezed out and crumbled, is a food much appreciated by most cockatiels of all ages; a generous teaspoonful a day is sufficient, fed separately from the seed. Green food should be fed daily, washed and wedged between the bars. Cabbage, lettuce, spinach, pieces of celery and wedges of carrot are all enjoyed. A piece of very clean cuttlefish bone is necessary too, tightly wedged between the bars of the cage. Mixed grit should be put on the floor or in a small container and frequently renewed. Good quality seed is most important since many illnesses result from dirty seed. For further information about feeding consult Chapter 8.

Cockatiels kept as pets need plenty of daily exercise outside their

Perches showing incorrect size (left) and correct (right).

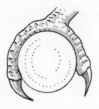

correct perching   incorrect perching

cages. They are strong flyers, but soon learn to fly round and round a room without banging their heads on the windows or flying into ornaments. They do not need toys – the affection and attention of their owner is much more important to them. Small branches of hazelnut, willow, or apple to chew however are very much appreciated (well washed and with the leaves removed). Most cockatiels will leave everything else for this natural food.

Very young children need to be watched closely if there is a pet cockatiel in the home. The reason is that they do not know their own strength and will often 'grab' the unsuspecting bird, and in trying to hold it, will squeeze it far too hard. This can result in the death of a much-loved pet, though there is always the exceptional five or six year old child who has real 'bird sense' and will quickly learn how to handle and look after a pet bird.

Hand-reared baby cockatiels will quickly learn to land on their owner, or go to some special place provided for them, but remember that any pet bird will fly straight out of an open door or window. In addition cockatiels that have been bought as adults will not make good pets, may bite hard, call loudly, and are very unlikely to settle down happily to cage life.

Accidents probably account for more deaths than illness in pet cockatiels. Owners of newly-acquired birds should remember that their pet does not know that fire burns, that gas flames burn, that ovens can be hot, and that water can be boiling. (See Chapter 11 for advice on first aid.) A victim of burning or scalding should immediately be splashed liberally with cold water, or held under a tap with cold running water for a few seconds. If this is done very quickly it will considerably lessen the burning or scalding. Next dry the bird very gently and return to its cage with something soft to stand on if its feet are affected.

If a cockatiel is badly shocked as a result of some accident, or some exceptional stress, give it a little glucose, or sugar, and water: about one eighth of a teaspoon of glucose or sugar to one teaspoon of lukewarm water. Two or three sips of this mixture at two hour intervals will help it to recover. A tiny piece of soft brown bread and milk may be appreciated. Usually birds recover from accidents in a few days unless they have been seriously hurt.

Cockatiels and cats do *not* mix, and the loser, possibly of its life, will be the cockatiel in any encounter between the two.

When a very young cockatiel is bought, a little help with feeding may make all the difference to its well-being. As mentioned before, seed should be spread over the floor at first, plus a little finely sieved grit. Many young birds refuse to eat because their throats have been scratched by trying to swallow a large sharp piece of grit.

For the first few weeks put a small earthenware water container on the floor of the cage. The bird will learn gradually to eat and drink out of seed and water containers fixed to the sides of the cage. Green food should be very finely cut up, and carrot should be grated finely; these latter foods should also go on the floor, fresh daily. Newly-acquired pet birds, especially if they are very young, need a lot of sleep, particularly mid-afternoon, and they need to be 'put to bed' early; 7 or 8 pm is late enough for a baby bird. A piece of dark-coloured material should be put over the cage for the night, which will allow it to sleep irrespective of lighted rooms. This will avoid many 'night frights'. A steady young cockatiel usually quickly adapts to home life and makes an endearing companion to every member of a family, or an affectionate and intelligent little friend to a single person.

A word of warning is necessary here about toxic fumes. Birds are extremely sensitive to all kinds of substances which are in daily use. The fumes from Teflon® pans and kitchenware coated with a similar substance can kill a cockatiel very fast. Teflon® is quite safe if properly used; but it is so easy to let a pan boil dry and that is when the damage is done. Gas fumes from leaking pipes can kill too, and smoke from a coal fire can cause serious injury. Canaries used to be taken down mines and when the bird collapsed, miners knew there were lethal fumes nearby. It is not generally known that various aerosol sprays, such as some hair sprays, for example, can cause problems for a pet bird. Needless to say, aerosols especially made for birds for various purposes are quite harmless, so long as the maker's instructions are followed.

Pet cockatiels should be covered up and put in a room with curtains drawn when fireworks are to be let off in the garden.

A newly-acquired pet cockatiel should be given a few days to settle down before any training operations are started. When the time comes, simply put a hand, palm downwards, into the perch beside the bird's feet. If it does not move away it is fairly tame and progress will be rapid. If it is nervous and panics all over the place, simply withdraw the hand, say some soothing words, or whistle;

18

then try again a few hours later. Do not put a hand into the cage of a young bird constantly if it is very nervous; 'Lessons' twice a day are enough for a baby. When it appears calm put one finger over the toes of the bird when it is on a perch, after a while it will step onto the finger. Keep practising this from time to time for a couple of days, then try drawing the hand out of the cage with the bird on the finger. As soon as it realises it is outside its cage it will probably panic and fly headlong into the first window it sees, knock its head hard and fall down. Pick it up immediately and soothe and calm it, letting it feel the warmth of two hands; then return it to the cage and try again later.

Cockatiels are extremely intelligent, and quickly learn 'house manners' such as avoiding windows and flying round a room rather than up and down, thus avoiding bangs on the head through bad 'landings'. It is not at all difficult to teach young cockatiels to fly from the hand round a room and back onto the shoulder.

Like all parrots and parakeets cockatiels love television and will sit quietly watching it for long periods and as with all birds, music tends to calm them. A young bird on its own needs a wealth of affection from its owner but this does *not* mean allowing the bird to put its beak near or in the owner's mouth to take 'tit-bits'. This habit should most certainly be avoided. The owner is not at all likely to be harmed by the contact with a healthy cockatiel, but the bird will certainly be subjected by this means to germs which may be harmless to humans, but will be damaging to its health.

I have only owned one talking cockatiel, and that only for a short time. He was a charming bird, but he would keep repeating a nursery rhyme all day long. Remember, be extremely careful what a prospective talker is allowed to hear. Once a cockatiel finds he can talk, he will enjoy himself repeating everything he has been taught, and a lot else besides.

When teaching a bird how to speak, speak loud and clear, and not too fast. It is after all a strange and difficult language for a bird to master. Avoid teaching 'nonsense'; it may be funny for a while, but it will be trying when constantly repeated over years. Give the bird a name which is easy for him to say.

The letter H is very difficult for a parrot-type bird to pronounce. B and J are easy. Names ending in Y or IE seem to be easiest. For example, Berty, Johnny and Joey are extremely easy for a cockatiel to master. Harold, on the other hand, would be difficult, and so would a name such as Ian; there is not enough 'sound' in it for the bird to pick up easily.

After their own name, the first 'sentence' a young bird can learn easily is 'very good' . Many of my colony aviary birds say these two words because they hear me say it to them in the morning. A sentence such as 'Joey very good', once mastered, will be uttered with every possible intonation which the owner of the bird has ever produced in his or her voice for any reason whatsoever. I well remember a pet cockatiel owned by a friend. This bird had a great sense of humour and was also extremely mischievous; after doing something particularly awful he would always say in a loud voice 'Berty is a *very* good boy'.

HENS

Although there are many talented female speakers amongst larger parrot-type birds, this seems to be rare with cockatiels. On the other hand, hens often make gentle and charming pets, but there is always the risk of egg binding with a hen cockatiel kept in a cage, however much calcium she gets. A hen is also quite likely to call frequently for a mate. A pair of pet cockatiels can be truly wonderful companions. Their affection for each other, assuming they are compatible, is charming to see, and in no way diminishes their love for their owner.

Pet cockatiels once past the 'baby' stage of up to ten weeks of age, should be given the opportunity for daily exercise outside their cage. It is also important to give any cockatiels kept indoors frequent (twice weekly) sprays with luke warm water. They enjoy this enormously and will spread out their wings like great butterflies to get the greatest possible amount of water from the spray. A small 'mist' spray used for indoor plants is best.

Many cockatiels like to 'paddle' in a shallow dish of water. They do this in the wild state, 'waddling' about in streams up to their middles in water, and breeding birds will always go down to thoroughly dampen their undersides when sitting on eggs. This brings very necessary humidity to their clutch of incubating eggs.

2 Colours, Mutations and Sexing

THE WILD OR NORMAL COCKATIEL

In the wild the cockatiel has a grey or greyish-brown coloured body with white median and secondary wing coverts, giving a broad white stripe down the wing. The primary wing feathers are dark grey, becoming black towards the tips. The eyes are brown, the beak dark grey, and the legs and feet blackish-grey. The cock has brilliant orange-red ear patches surrounded by yellow, blending into a white edge around the face. The underside of the tail is dark grey to black, and the feathers of the crest are yellow tipped with grey.

The hen has much duller ear patches surrounded by grey and the crest is grey. The undersides of the tail feathers are striped, with yellow outer feathers and the undersides are covered in white or yellowish spots.

The sex of adult birds therefore is visually obvious, but the young are not so easy to define. Both cock and hen young are pale editions of the hen; cocks will start to show yellow colour on their faces at about six months of age. Full adult colouring takes about one year, and varies according to the time of year the birds are hatched. Birds bred early in the year will moult out sooner than those bred later on.

Normal-looking birds can vary in colour. Some with almost black wings could well be Pearl cocks that have reverted; others bred from matings of mutations could be split for a recessive colour that cannot be seen. Unfortunately, when breeding for colour, mutation will not only produce the colour but very often affects other parts of the bird's anatomy, resulting in lack of size, stance, poor crests, short legs and poor eyesight.

Beauty, as ever, is in the eye of the beholder, and for many the pure bred normal bird, with its size, stance and crest (many three inches high) is the ideal cockatiel. Such normals are very often amongst the winners at shows in the USA.

MUTATIONS

By the year 1860 cockatiels were becoming well known as pets and large numbers were being caught in the wild in Australia and exported. Records show that by 1884 the cockatiel was established as a breeding bird in Europe, but it was most popular in the USA and it was there that the majority of the birds were sent. However, this trade ceased in 1960 when the Australian government placed an embargo on the export of wild caught birds.

In the wild birds seldom mutate, and if they do, they rarely survive. It is not surprising, threfore, that during the first hundred years of their popularity, colour mutations in cockatiels were practically unknown. However, with the cessation of imports, and the free breeding nature of the birds, inbreeding was taking place, leading to colour mutations. The fact that the largest numbers of birds were kept in the USA at the time is no doubt the reason that the earlier colour mutations occurred in this area. Unfortunately the genetics providing the colours were not properly understood at that time. The keeping of records seems to have been non-existent, so it took a long time for breeders to understand and evolve proper breeding programmes to establish a strain.

There are seven colour mutations arising from two different types of chromosomes mutating; one is sex-linked and the other autosomal, which is known as recessive.

Sex-Linked	Recessive
Cinnamon	Fallow
Lutino	Pied
Pearl	Silver
	White faced

Whilst the Lutino remains an all-time favourite, combinations of the above mutations provide the popular:

Cinnamon-Pearl
Cinnamon-Pied
Cinnamon-Pearl-Pied
Lutino-Pearl
Lutino-Pearl-Pied

Since 1981 a further factor, discovered in the UK, has been added to mutations: a silver strain with dominant silver genes. This is the first dominant colour mutation known in cockatiels, and will no doubt pave the way for new mutations in the future.

As genetics and carefully controlled breeding programmes became understood, birds in the new colours were more freely available, and rarity became sought-after by cockatiel enthusiasts.

Colours started to come in different shades, breeders began to elaborate on their colour descriptions, and in order that rules could be laid down for these colour variations, in March 1983 The Parrot Society of the UK held a meeting with breeders of mutation cockatiels. The major questions settled at this meeting concerned the definitions to be used for the various amounts of yellow carried in some mutations, and whether there was sufficient difference between Pearled and Laced markings to warrant them being described separately.

It was decided that two shades of yellow existed in addition to Lutino, namely Primrose and Buttercup. There were some misgivings regarding the use of Buttercup and it was agreed that this description should be used sparingly as very few birds could match up to this standard , and members would need to substantiate the use of this name by the quality of colour present in their birds.

It was established that Lutinos, Cinnamons and Pieds would be covered by the following names.

Lutino: Primrose Lutino, Buttercup Lutino
Cinnamon: Primrose Cinnamon, Buttercup Cinnamon
Pied: Primrose Pied, Buttercup Pied

It was also decided that there was sufficient difference between the Pearl and Lacewing to warrant distinctive names being applied, although care in the use of the term Lacewing was very necessary as with many birds the markings fall between the two.

It was established that when describing a combination of Pearl and Lacewing with Lutino it will be described as Lutino Pearl and Lutino Lacewing, without any mention of the amount of yellow present. It was also established that the name Cinnamon should precede Pied, Lutino, Lacewing, etc., when describing combinations that include Cinnamon.

THE SEX-LINKED MUTATIONS
Cinnamon (often called Isabella in Europe)
With the exception of the grey colour being replaced with brown (cinnamon) both Cinnamon cocks and hens are similar to the normals. For the first few weeks their young have paler eyes than the normal, sometimes looking a reddish colour. The feet and legs are pinkish. In the adult birds the Cinnamon colour varies. It can sometimes be very light and the cocks are darker than the hens. Sexing is straightforward after the first moult, as with the normals.

Cinnamon was the second of the sex-linked mutations to appear. It was first discovered in Belgium. This probably happened in the early 1960s as it was reported as an established breeding mutation there in 1967.

Lutino
This is the best and most popular mutation that has so far been produced. Because of its all-white appearance and its red eyes, pink feet and skin, it was originally called Albino or White. But as these birds have yellow crests, red-orange cheek patches and carry a varying amount of yellow plumage (the deeper the yellow the more they are sought after) they cannot be Albinos. Adult birds also develop a pale lavender diffusion on the wing coverts. Albinos are pure white birds, devoid of yellow, or any other colour, with no yellow crescent or cheek patches.

Mr George A. Smith, the well known veterinarian in aviculture, explains the effects of the colouring agent melanin in his book *Encyclopedia of Cockatiels*.

23

Many Lutinos still carry a genetic fault, which has been passed down for nearly thirty years: a clear patch is visible at the back of the head. Do not accept over preening or feather plucking as the reason, it is inherited baldness which will not go away. An otherwise good bird should not be rejected for this reason but, of course, until bred out, the heredity fault will continue.

Efforts have been made to breed a deep 'Buttercup Yellow' strain without a great deal of success to date, as it seems that breeding for intensity in this colour, and mating birds with a similar depth of colour, has so far only brought out genetic faults such as feather problems and weakness, which has precluded the development of a satisfactory strain. However, breeders will continue to make great efforts to overcome the problems as a deep yellow would be the ideal coloured cockatiel for so many keepers.

It should be noted that when breeding for double mutations the Lutino colour will override and mask some other colours, particularly Cinnamon, and a Lutino Pied appears no different to a Lutino.

Sexing used to be considered easy because primrose spots under the wings denoted a hen. But this has in many cases proved to be incorrect, as some cocks when young have similar markings. The most certain way of sexing is to wait for the constant singing of the young cocks. This usually occurs between three and six months of age. It must be remembered that young hens will also often sing for a short period of time, but never continuously like the cocks.

Lutino was the second mutation to be discovered, and the first of the sex-linked colours. Records published give details of how this new colour was produced from a seemingly normal pair of birds owned by Mr Cliff Barringer in Florida, USA in 1958. They were subsequently acquired by Mrs E. L. Moon, well known aviculturist, who at one time was curator of Parrot Jungle in Florida. It was Mrs Moon who undertook the hard work of developing the strain which attained such a world-wide appeal.

These birds were first introduced into the UK in 1968. Two pairs were acquired from Mrs Moon by Mr Reg Partridge and Mr E. Pariente. Mr Pariente had been curator of Elbourne Zoo and at the time was living in a flat at Brighton, and as arrangements to house the new birds had not been completed they were first housed and looked after by Mr Ken Dolton, the well known aviculturist, in his aviaries at Worcester.

Pearled and Lacewing
These are extremely attractive birds, and until moulted out the appearance of both cocks and hens is similar. They have orange-red ear patches, their faces are yellow flecked with grey, and the crests are yellow streaked with grey. The feathers right down from the

back of the neck, the shoulders and often also the breast have a scalloped appearance, the white or yellow feathers being edged in grey, with grey or yellow centres, and there is a white band down the edge of the wings. Both sexes are mottled and spotted underneath the wings, and the upper part of the primaries are primrose yellow blending into dark brown at the ends. The cock is yellow streaked with grey with the underside striped and dappled with yellow and grey. There is a big variation in both the yellow colour and feather pattern. Those with heavy pearl markings with an elongated effect, right down from the back of the neck, are now termed Lacewings. Genetically there is no difference; they have been selectively bred to consistently produce the laced effect.

Birds with a deep yellow colour are often called Golden Pearls and those with white pearling are called Silver or Dilute Pearls. When the young are in the nest, Pearls are most interesting for the nestlings vary in markings and colour, and it is always exciting to watch their development. Sexing is straightforward after the moult because whereas the hens retain their beautiful markings, the cocks lose theirs and revert to a charcoal colour, which appears like a very dark normal. By 1986 a strain had been developed and was being offered for sale in the USA where the cocks do not revert, but retain the pearled patterns.

This mutation was first developed in Germany in 1967, but was also occurring in other places at about the same time, as it was reported in Belgium in 1968.

The Pearled mutation has been widely used for breeding and establishing double mutations.

THE RECESSIVE (AUTOSOMAL) MUTATIONS
Fallow
Although the mode of inheritance is different, the Fallow is similar to the Cinnamon, but it has red eyes and the body colour is a much paler cinnamon, often two-toned, diffused with primrose yellow, with a golden yellow face colour. The most beautiful birds are to be found amongst the hens, as they are usually of a much lighter colour than the cocks. Sexing is not straightforward, because although the hens are usually paler there is such a variation in the shade of the colour that the only sure way is to watch for the constant singing of the cocks.

The first record of raising Fallows was in Florida, USA, in 1971. Mr Dale R. Thompson, Director, Aviculture Institute, Los Angeles, California, in an article '37 Years of Mutations' in the journal of the *National Cockatiel Society of America*, Volume III, July-August 1986, writes, 'The establishment of Fallows was in Florida by Mrs Irma Vowels. She raised one male in 1971, a second in 1972 and then two females in 1973'.

This mutation is kept mainly in the USA and few are available in the UK and Europe, but this position could change depending on the success of the breeding programmes where they are now being used to produce combined mutations.

Pied

This popular mutation is freely available. The best examples look outstandingly beautiful, especially in outdoor aviaries, but there is a big variation in piedness to the point of some looking nondescript. Both cocks and hens look the same, the ideal birds having seventy five per cent primrose yellow with twenty five per cent light or dark grey, the grey systematically and uniformly marked down each shoulder in the shape of a horseshoe. Feathers on the breast, the back and the flights and in the tail should be clear and no dark areas or spots should appear on the face or in the crest. Some people do like a grey band across the chest. However, some birds are very white in appearance, have very uneven markings, sooty faces, grey breasts and a mixture of light and dark coloured tail feathers. The worst examples are birds that are nearly all grey with a few white blotches, and people who have acquired such Pieds can hardly believe that theirs are of the same mutation when they see how striking and outstanding are the good specimens.

Good Pieds are termed heavy Pieds and the only way to obtain a strain is to selectively breed over several generations. Even so, uneven markings, although to a lesser degree, can still appear.

Sexing of Pieds is only possible by watching the behaviour of the birds. As young hens will often sing for a short period of time, it is a matter of waiting for the young cocks to sing continuously; they may start at six weeks, or they may wait for six months. Before six months has passed, many young hens will have been mated; this is a matter of having the time to watch, catch them up and fit a coloured plastic ring to identify them.

The Pied reported in California in 1949 was the first colour mutation to occur in cockatiels in aviculture. It seems that they were bred at the same time in Southern California by a Mr D. Putman and Mrs R. Kersh in different aviaries with no apparent connection. Mrs Kersh is reported to have acquired her founding bird from a pet shop. She worked very hard on the development of the mutation for over thirty years and it was from her birds that Europeans obtained most of their stock.

Silver

There are two completely different strains of this mutation, the first of which came from Europe and is now in the USA and to a lesser extent in the UK. These birds are of 'Recessive' (Autosomal) inheritance.

The other strain now being successfully bred in the UK is 'Dilute' and the birds' inheritance has come from different genes than those that have produced other colour mutations. They are 'Dominant' in this colour, and this is the first time a dominant colour mutation has appeared in cockatiels.

Recessive Silver
The difference between normal and Recessive Silver birds is that the eye colour in the Silver is red, and the grey feathers are replaced with those of a silvery colour. As in the normals the depth of colour varies, and whilst some appear a light silver, the shading in others can appear almost fallow or cinnamon. The body colour of the hen is similar to that of the cock: yellow areas are faintly tinted, and the underside of the tail is striped with yellow and silver-grey. The method of sexing is the same as with the normals.

Cockatiels of 'Silver-Grey' colour were first reported from New Zealand in the early 1950s, but as they were not established as a fixed mutation, it appears that they did not survive. The first records of a new mutation came from Europe in the late 1960s; but it was a sad story, as the young being bred in Germany, Holland and Belguim all had other genetic faults associated with the colour and at first nearly all were blind. It has since taken nearly ten years of dedicated work on the part of the breeders to try to eliminate the problems, which always seem to be associated with red-eyes.

Dominant Silver (Dilute)
In this mutation, the grey colour of the normal bird is diluted to give a silvery pastel shade, the yellow is retained on the face and the front of the head, the orange-red cheek patches appear to be brighter, the eyes are black and the legs are grey. As with the normal birds the depth of colour varies, from a shade lighter on the hen to a beautiful silvery-white on the cock, with all birds showing a darker shade on the head and neck. When the young appear from the nest there is no way of sexing them, as they all look the same, having a pale grey-brownish-brick colour, with a darker grey on the head and neck giving a skull cap appearance. Otherwise they look like normals, although the yellow colour is stronger.

At the first moult there is little change in the appearance of the hen, although the grey becomes lighter and the yellow a little brighter, with an enhanced colour of the cheek patches. The cock, however, is transformed. It takes on a silvery-grey appearance, and all traces of the brownish-brick colour disappear. The depth of colour varies; some cocks can become very light, while others are marked as normals, but with a yellow wash all over the bird, with an intensification of the cheek patches, and the yellow on the head. The darker grey skull cap remains present.

Double Factor

The genes in the Dominant Silver cockatiel produce two visual effects in either a single or double quantity, known as single or double factor. Similar colour effects are well known in budgerigars and lovebirds. The double factor brings a further dilution, giving an almost yellowish-white appearance to the head and wings, with a wash of grey. The eyes are black, and the legs are grey.

The history of this mutation started in 1979, when Mr Terry Cole, a market gardener and cockatiel enthusiast from Swindon, saw and bought an unusually silver-coloured cock bird from a pet shop. As it had been bred from parents that were visually normal the possibility arose that it could be a new 'Dominant' mutation. Fortunately, being an experienced breeder, Mr Cole was able to plan and keep records of his breeding programmes, and equally importantly had the space to build the very many extra aviaries that were eventually required. Ably supported by his friend, Mr Mike Gunston, it took six years to establish the strain.

For those interested in the joys, trials and tribulations of breeding a new mutation, the following details are extracts from Mr Cole's breeding records.

'The cock was first paired with a Lutino hen. Nine young were bred, all looking normal, so this was a setback of my thoughts of a 'Dominant' bird. A search then made for the parents of the cock revealed that the cock had died, but the hen was acquired. In 1980 mother was mated to son, and of the thirteen cocks and hens bred, three cocks were dilutes; all the others were of normal appearance.

'The 1981-2 breeding programme included inbreeding, and the introduction of unrelated blood to build up the size and strength, to avoid weakness that has beset other mutations. Results over this period were now most encouraging and pointed to the incidence of double and single factor in the colour. It took a further three years and many more aviaries, to build up the picture and prove the genetic mutation, being late 1985, early 1986 when the pairing of Silver to Cinnamon produced three silvers and seven normals, and mating a Silver to Pearl/Pied produced three Silvers and one normal proved the 'Dominant' inheritance of my Silvers.'

White Faced

This mutation differs from other mutations as it does not have the orange-red cheek patches, and does not carry any yellow at all, so the birds are coloured mainly black with a varying amount of grey and white. The wings carry a white stripe as in the normals, and the eyes are dark in colour. In the USA they were originally called 'Charcoal' because of their sooty appearance. Both sexes have the same grey heads before the first moult. After the moult the cock's face becomes white, the crest being grey streaked with white, whilst the hen remains grey, often with a suffusion of white on the face, with the crest grey and the underneath of the tail feathers mottled in white.

The first White Faced could well have been bred in Europe in the early 1970s. There had been recollections of them in Holland and West Germany. Records show the first appearance in 1979, both in Holland and the UK at about the same time. Mr N. D. Cooper, chairman of the Parrot Society in the UK, acquired the first bird seen in this country. He developed the strain and its history is well documented. Mr Cooper wrote an article 'The White Faced Cockatiel' in the September 1981 issue of the *Magazine of The Parrot Society*, Volume XV, No.9.

This mutation is now being combined with other mutations, which may well in due course lead to the introduction of some new strains. In 1986 we started to see advertisements appear in the specialist cockatiel journals or magazines offering for sale triple splits to Cinnamon-Pearl and Pied.

COMBINED MUTATIONS

With selective matings of single, double and treble mutations, it was theoretically possible by the mid-1960s to breed at least fifty mutations whose colours could be visually identified; although many would of course only be differences in shades of the same colour. New mutations will no doubt continue to appear, and it is this aspect of breeding which interests and appeals to so many cockatiel enthusiasts.

Below are some descriptions of the most popular combinations of the mutations.

Cinnamon-Pearl

This is basically a Cinnamon bird with the pearling or lacing spreading from the back of the neck, down through the wing coverts, but not on the tail feathers; the breast can also be pearled. Pearling on the feathers can vary from being edged with a very light brown, almost silver, with a white background, to a deeper colour of edging with a background of golden yellow, which is usually described as Primrose Cinnamon Pearl. This latter effect on a Lacewing bird gives a very striking appearance. Although the hens retain their pearling, on the cock it is gradually lost as the moult takes place, reverting to an attractive grey colour.

Cinnamon-Pied

The appearance of these birds is the same as the Pied, except that the grey area is replaced by the cinnamon colour. Even marking and the lack of flecking or spots is desirable. The influence of cinnamon often produces a good primrose colour. Although the hens tend to be larger than the cocks, sexing can only be established by the constant singing of the cocks.

Cinnamon-Pearl-Pied
This is considered by many to be the most beautiful mutation, with the combination of cinnamon pearl or lacing and the light colour ranging from white to a lovely primrose. Symmetrical, even marking, with clear back, front and tail feathers is the ideal, as for the Pied. Some people like pearling across the back, in the form of a necklace, with a band of cinnamon across the chest. Viewed at close quarters the Primrose Lacewing Pied is without doubt a most outstanding bird.

The cock loses his pearling at the moult, reverting to the attractive fawn, yellow or white, of a Pied cockatiel. As with other Pieds, the only sure way to sex is by the singing of the cocks.

Pearl Pied
The colours of this mutation are the same as those of the Pied, the only difference being that the grey areas of feather are pearled. Some enthusiasts prefer a larger area of these markings down the wings to that of the ideal Pied, in order to show off the lovely pearling. The hens retain their pearling, but most cocks revert to Pied at the first moult, although some retain their pearling for several years. Some breeders in the USA are advertising strains of which they say that the cocks retain their pearling and do not revert to Pied.

Lutino Pearl
This is one of the most beautiful mutations of any so far produced in cockatiels. It is in the mature hens that one sees an almost 'golden' bird; a really good Lutino Pearl hen with deep gold pearling, fusing into the clear yellow of the rest of her body is 'quite a bird'. Like all other mutations, individual specimens vary enormously; some are Lutino (white) with gold pearling on the back and shoulders, almost white wing and tail feathers, but of course retaining a golden yellow crest and orange-red ear patches. Others are truly yellow all over except for the large orange-red ear patches. Their crests, wings, the whole of the body and especially tails are a deep clear yellow with golden pearling on the back and shoulders. The eyes are red at first, as in the Lutino. The cocks revert to Lutino, which is very useful for sexing, while the hens retain their pearling.

The popularity of these lovely birds could well overtake that of the Lutino, since they do not appear to acquire the slightly 'dusty' look down the back, known as 'Lavender wash' which afflicts Lutinos.

The Lutino Pearl has been bred in Europe and the USA since the early 1970s. The most prolific strain in the UK was developed by Mr

R. Whitby, a well-known breeder from Wales. It took him four years to develop his strain, starting with a pair of normal split for Pearl birds in 1972. From their offspring the Pearl hens were mated to Lutino cocks. The resulting splits were then bred with Pearls and Lutinos to eventually produce Pearled Lutinos, which is the name preferred by Mr Whitby.

Lutino Pearl Pied
This mutation is visually the same as the Lutino Pearl, although many breeders claim that the inclusion of Pied in this mutation produces a deeper yellow colour. Perhaps the biggest break-through will come when cocks are bred which retain their colour, and do not revert. No doubt it will not be long before breeders turn their attention to producing such an attractive mutation in numbers sufficient to popularise them. Lutino Pearl Pieds are available in the USA and are strikingly beautiful birds of perfect proportions. They retain their red eyes.

Albino
These are pure white birds with red eyes, devoid of any yellow, without even the yellow crest or coloured cheek' patches. This mutation was obtained by a protracted breeding programme of White Faced to Lutino. The first breeding appears to have taken place in Europe in the Netherlands in 1980. The first breeding in the USA was reported in 1985.

THE FUTURE OF MUTATIONS
There are bound to be more new mutations or combinations of existing mutations in the coming years. We are always hearing and reading of new combinations on the way, and who knows what may appear in a pet shop?

3 Avoiding Difficulties with Local and State Authorities; Security; Transport

Those who intend to keep cockatiels in built-up areas should find out the attitude of their local governing bodies or councils before embarking on expensive building projects. Many people may well protest that if they consulted every person or body who might conceivably be at some time concerned, they would never even start to keep birds. This may be true, but failing to consider the necessary requirements may cause just as many problems in the long term. Perhaps a 'middle' course is the one which some prospective owners may decide to take.

The middle way has worked well in all but a few unfortunate cases. It consists of finding out what are the requirements of the area, or in the USA, finding out what are the State Laws, and arranging any aviary buildings to comply as nearly as possible with these requirements. In the event of a complaint of any kind it can then be shown that the owner has done everything in his or her power to comply with the local or State regulations.

US State laws prohibiting the keeping of birds obviously cannot be circumvented until or unless they are rescinded. The American Federation of Aviculture, or A.F.A. as it is known, gives information on the State legislation already in existence or on laws shortly to come into use. Information is also provided about possible future legislation, so that objections can be made if necessary.

In the United Kingdom local bye-laws are another matter. Many have fallen into disuse, and most District and Local Councils will turn a blind eye if everything possible has been done to comply with normal requirements of light, hygiene and appearance. This means that an individual must not, by building, take light from a neighbour's room, and houses and flights should not be more than 6ft 3in (two metres) high. No building to house birds should be placed in immediate proximity to a dwelling house, either one's own, or a neighbours. No building should be erected in such a way that it may be deemed to be an 'eyesore', in other words to denigrate the area, or detract from its overall appearance and it would be unwise to more than half fill a garden with aviaries.

In Great Britain it must be remembered that many councils forbid the keeping of animals and birds on their estates. Others are not so inflexible, but they do require notice of any building to be erected.

Some private estates of houses and some blocks of apartments forbid the keeping of animals and birds altogether.

The old established custom whereby residents of long standing in a particular area could claim immunity from complaints by newer residents on the grounds that: 'There never has been a complaint, so it must be alright', no longer applies. An individual may be happily and peacefully keeping birds, and animals for many years, when suddenly a new neighbour moves in next door, decides that he or she does not like birds or wants to make a case that there is a nuisance in order to try to get their rates reduced, and the unfortunate owner of the birds can in theory be brought to court.

Unless the owner of the birds can prove that the case was groundless, he or she may find themselves instructed by a magistrate to drastically reduce the number of birds kept, or even to get rid of them altogether. Such a situation would be likely to arise only if the birds were grossly overcrowded, and quite inadequately cared for and managed; and where the owner had not taken due regard of the fact that a lot of birds together do at times make a lot of noise.

By far the best defence against unfair harassment is scrupulous attention to hygiene, no overcrowding, siting the aviaries as far as possible from neighbours' houses and enlisting the support and sympathy of other neighbours.

Most people who make complaints will avoid going as far as taking the matter to court: the cost is considerable, and the waiting time can be long. The average person will usually think again if they are approached and talked to sympathetically, and their own 'nuisance making' is quietly pointed out. There is always something one neighbour is doing which might annoy another.

People intent on making a complaint go first to their local council. When they receive a visit the council will probably send along a representative, sometimes accompanied by a representative from the Ministry of Environment. These individuals are usually well aware of the diverse reasons which cause neighbours to complain, not least the desire to pay less in rates. When the representatives are invited in to view the premises and aviaries, if all is well kept and the birds appear contented, they will almost certainly inform the owner 'There is no cause for complaint here'. If this is the outcome, it is a good idea to tell all neighbours, as public opinion has a strong influence on fairmindedness in such a situation.

SECURITY

Cockatiels have to combat many predators. To understand this, one has only to watch a large colony of thirty or forty cockatiels living together react to hawks, cats, etc. All will be quiet and peace, but somewhere amongst that crowd of sleepy-looking birds is one or more 'guard'; their vigilant eye spots a hawk perhaps, high above, coming out of the sun. In a split second all hell is let loose, as a milling mass of flapping wings makes it impossible for the predator to distinguish any one individual bird. Such behaviour is all very well during the day, but at night a great deal of damage can be created by the birds panicking. In built-up areas where neighbours' cats can cause tremendous losses by just sitting on the roof of a flight, the best answer is to roof the flight and double wire the sides.

There is also an excellent cat and fox 'scarer' on the market, which does the animals no harm but gives them a twelve volt shock; enough to stop them jumping on the roofs of aviaries. It is not difficult to erect, and can be run off a battery; or it can be connected to mains electricity supplies. It is called 'Cracker Jack' and can be bought at some of the larger establishments selling birds, seeds and aviaries.

Those who have valuable collections of birds will be well advised to consider installing one of the many security systems available. The options are numerous. Pressure mats, heat seeking beams, search lights, alarm bells wired to the owner's home, all have their uses. Perhaps the best arrangement is a combination of all the above.

Many security systems are complicated and need a highly specialised technician to install them. The more complicated systems also need once or twice yearly inspection and servicing. The expense of installing really effective protection from bird thieves is well worth while when one considers the frequency with which birds are stolen. There are many large companies specialising in the installation of alarm systems; but some people may prefer to go to a relatively small local firm, run by one or two highly trained people. In this case, if anything goes wrong with the system after it is installed, and perhaps the guarantee has run out, someone will arrive to investigate who probably knows exactly how the system was laid out, where everything is to be found and what is likely to be wrong. The cost of rectifying the fault will then be much less than that charged by a large company employing many people, who cannot possibly know exactly how each system was laid.

TRANSPORTING BIRDS IN THE UK
SENDING COCKATIELS BY RAIL
Cockatiels travel extremely well by the three most usual means of transport – road, rail and air. Probably by far the greatest number of privately-owned birds which are either sold or exchanged in Great Britain travel by Red Star British Rail. If you intend to send birds by rail for any reason, it is well worth a visit to a rail station to pick up the Red Star timetable for the year in question. This sets out the best station for sending livestock. British Rail is, on the whole, a fast and efficient mode of transport for birds, provided that care is taken with the timing of their arrival at the station of departure. If birds have a

journey of over 200 miles, it is much better to take them to the departure station in the afternoon, so that they will travel overnight. A 'phone call should be made the night before departure to warn the buyer to be ready to collect as early as possible. Red Star will only handle livestock from Mondays to Thursdays inclusive, so it is obviously not wise to send birds on a very long journey on a Thursday, which might mean them arriving on a Friday, thus causing difficulties for the rail staff.

Most British Rail staff take great care of birds, but they do like boxes to be strong and properly secured. Cockatiels travel very well in very strong cardboard boxes especially made for the purpose of rail travel. These can be bought at various establishments catering for equipment for birds. The birds will be much more comfortable if the floor of the box is lined with corrugated cardboard, as this prevents their feet slipping during movement.

Cockatiels, or any birds, being transported even quite short distances, should always be given at least three days' supply of seed. Water should not be put in the boxes; it will spill and if the boxes are cardboard they will be seriously damaged. If they are wooden boxes the water will form a puddle and the birds will get in a terrible mess. If cockatiels are given the chance to drink just before transportation that is all that is necessary.

Although the British Rail label does state the station to which the birds are going, etc., it is also necessary for the sender to print clearly the name, address and telephone number of the buyer, plus clear instructions if the birds are to be called for by the new owner (designated 'the consignee' on British Rail forms). Red waterproof marking pens are best for addressing boxes.

Before sending birds away, always check that their rings are loose and comfortable. Newcomers to bird keeping do not always realise the intense distress a plastic or metal ring can cause if it is too tight. Any such rings should be removed before the birds are railed.

TRANSPORT BY AIR

Birds to be exported or sent very long distances are best sent by air. Only certain airlines deal with the transportation of birds. If the birds are to be exported, say, from the United Kingdom, the first step is to get in touch with the nearest branch of the Ministry of Agriculture and Fisheries. They will inform the prospective exporter what other Authorities must be contacted for certificates of health and any other requirements for the importation of birds to the specified country. The embassy of the country concerned will probably be the next to be contacted. Certificates of health will certainly be necessary, perhaps from a veterinarian specified by the Ministry of Agriculture; usually a local veterinarian will be able to arrange the necessary visits to the exporter's premises.

Airline Freight Departments usually require about 48 hours' notice of arrival of birds for transportation abroad. Boxes *must* comply with their requirements; these boxes are called IATA (International Air Transport Association) boxes. In the United Kingdom, Southern Aviaries, Hadlow Down, Sussex, supply them.

ROAD TRANSPORT

There are companies which transport birds by road, but the expense is so high that it is only worth while for the most expensive of birds.

IMPORTATION OF COCKATIELS TO THE UNITED KINGDOM

Again, the local branch of the Ministry of Agriculture and Fisheries must be contacted for an import licence. It will probably also be necessary to apply to the Ministry of Environment for permission to import birds. The birds will have to be quarantined. During those weeks of quarantine a veterinarian, either local, or appointed by one of the Ministries, will have to have free access to inspect the birds at any time, and any number of times, at the importer's or new owner's expense.

4   Housing

When considering the acquisition of cockatiels, and the provision of an aviary, it is important to first read Chapter 3 on general management. Decisons must then be taken on the type of aviary required, where it will be sited, and what furnishings will be needed for both house and flight. Should provision be made for any desirable extras, such as lighting, dimmer switches and controls, security, etc? Also very important is looking to the future; enthusiasts nearly always like to acquire more birds, so will the site and aviary lend themselves to alterations or additions? These various aspects are considered under the following headings.

THE AVIARY SITE
Much will of course depend on whether one is living in a built-up or country area. If the area is built-up, neighbours must be taken into account, for although cockatiels are generally quiet, docile and friendly birds, they do call for short periods, morning and evening. Moreover cockatiels like and will benefit from sitting in the sun, so a flight facing south would be ideal; if this is impossible, locate it where the sun will shine at some time of the day.

SELECTING AN AVIARY
The ideal size for one pair of cockatiels is a house of plan size 3ft × 3ft (approx. 1m square), 6ft (2m) high with a flight 3ft (1m) wide, 9ft (3m) long by 6ft (2m) high. There is always a great deal of competition between aviary manufacturers, so study what is on offer. If possible, view them to make comparisons, but remember

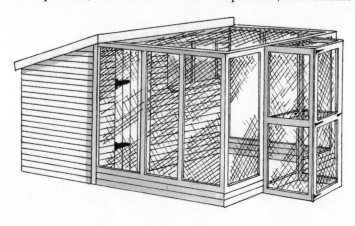

A typical aviary for two pairs of cockatiels.

the least expensive may well have smaller sizes of timber that will not be as durable.

To keep two pairs of birds, the house size for one pair is satisfactory, but the width of the flight should be increased to 6ft (2m). One nest box should be placed in the house and the other in the flight.

SAFETY PORCHES
It must be stressed that most standard aviaries do not include safety porches; they are usually extras. Low entrance doors are provided to enter the flights, based on a theory that the birds will not fly low and escape. In practice this does not always work, so safety porches are considered essential. Full sized doors in porch and flight give easy access for persons, boxes, cages, food, etc., and how much easier and less stressful it is to catch a bird in the small confine of the porch, rather than in the flight.

To keep a colony of cockatiels that will look very attractive, the octagonal aviary shown in the colour section is ideal; this will comfortably hold four breeding pairs. An additional benefit and a big advantage of this type of aviary is that by using flight panels, one with a door, part of the flight can be temporarily segregated to house young birds.

For those who wish to have a number of aviaries that will blend in with and at the same time enhance the appearance of their garden, an illustration is shown in the colour section of two blocks of aviaries, with a path, and flowerbeds in between.

For those who wish to keep and breed a large number of birds, but whose time is limited, another illustration is shown of a block with a spanned roof house. The centre aisle running through the house allows for feeding without entering the individual aviaries.

When planning aviaries for cockatiel breeding it must be borne in mind that separate accommodation will be necessary for young birds, as those from an early nest will often interfere, with damaging results, with the young in a second nest.

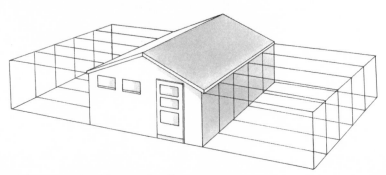

A block of aviaries with spanned roof house.

PREPARING FOR THE ERECTION OF THE AVIARY

To exclude vermin, and for good hygiene, the house should be erected on a concrete base. To keep the house above the floor level of the flight a depth of 6 in (15 cm) is recommended. Lay on a foundation of rubble and use one part cement to four parts coarse sand or fine gravel. When shuttering to take the cement make sure the base will be straight and level, and allow the house to overlap slightly on all sides to ensure that rainwater will not run underneath. To provide a damp course lay a sheet of pliable polythene or PVC over the cement when approximately 4 in (10cm) has been laid, and continue to fill up to the top of the shuttering. To avoid problems from gale force winds it is advisable to secure the house to the base using rawlplugs and plated screws.

Grass or gravel under flights not only entails a lot of work in keeping clean, but before long will become so fouled as to need replacement. It is better to use paving stones, which are freely available in many sizes at garden centres. Laying on a bed of sand makes them easy to level. leave $\frac{1}{4}$ in (0.63cm) between each for drainage, and to exclude mice. Edges should protrude slightly outside the flight panels, which as they are progressively erected should be secured to the paving stones, using rawlplugs and plated screws.

FURNISHING THE AVIARY

Although cockatiels are very hardy birds, and do not require heat in the winter, they should be made more comfortable by insulating the

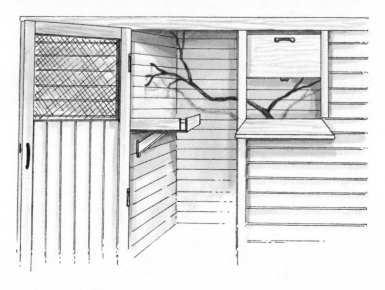

Interior of small house.

roof of the house if they are to be kept in a very cold area. It is not difficult to cut a sheet of plywood to fit the inside of the ceiling, and fix in position with a sandwich of suitable insulating material with a width of not less than 2in (5cm).

Protection from north and east winds should be given in the winter. Plastic sheeting can be fixed to the flight panels, but it is better to make detachable screens although initially more expensive, using a lightweight framework onto which is screwed a thin sheet of rigid PVC. These last are simple to fit and easy to store.

Cockatiels will flap about at the slightest disturbance – other people's cats seem to be a common problem, and, although enjoying a shower, they do not like heavy downfalls of rain, so it is best to cover the roof of the flight with transparent or translucent roofing sheets. To fully protect the birds, double wiring of the flight panels is advisable. The outside wire need only be loosely attached and to ensure a gap wooden spacers can be inserted where necessary. Blackening of the wire makes the birds much easier to see, and more importantly, makes it easier for the birds to see *you*. Brush or roll on bitumastic paint, both sides of the outside wire, but before fitting do not forget to treat the existing wire.

If electricity is available, lighting is very helpful; a low or dimmed light on all night ensures that the birds can get back to their perch if disturbed, and feeding time is extended. There is a wide choice of dimmers, controls, and timeswitches available, but unless you have a good understanding of electrics, be sure to employ an electrician for the installation.

A perch should be fitted across the house near the back. It is important that this perch be positioned higher than any fitted in the flight, as birds roost on the highest point. Perches used should be of different diameters, ranging from $\frac{5}{8}$ in (1.6cm) to 1 in (2.54cm). Several should be fixed in the flight.

Most houses are fitted with entrance traps, or popholes, which will be of maximum convenience if they can be closed and opened from the outside of the aviary. A shelf to take the feeding utensils should be mounted underneath the windows in the house. It should be large enough to accommodate the extra containers which will be needed at breeding time.

A convenient way to fix pieces of apple, carrot, etc., is by hammering two nails about 1 in (2.54cm) apart into a perch. Green food can be attached to the perches by twisting over with a piece of thin wire.

Nest boxes are available in many sizes. The ideal size is internal measurements of 9in × 9in (22.7cm square) by 15in (38cm) deep, made from wood $\frac{3}{4}$ in (1.9cm) thick. The entrance hole should be 3in (7.6cm) diameter and have $\frac{5}{8}$"(1.6cm) diameter perch, protruding both inside and outside fitted 1in (2.54cm) below the hole. The

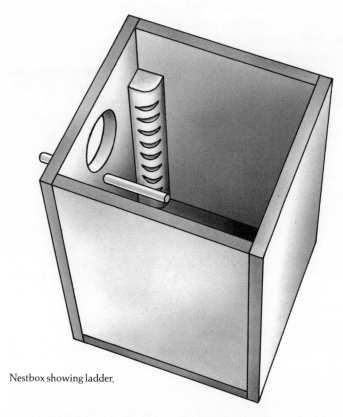

Nestbox showing ladder.

picture of the nestbox shows a ladder which has been found to be ideal; renewable, secured by two screws from the outside, it is set down to the bottom of the box and, keeps the birds contented whilst in the nest, as they like to chew on the wood.

SOME HINTS WHEN MAKING AN AVIARY
An important consideration is the width of the flight; nearly all commercially made flights are in 36 in (1m) wide modules. In practice, when entering aviaries of this width, the birds immediately fly down to the other end, but we have found that both cockatiels and other birds will stay on a longitudinal perch and become much steadier in a width of 48 in (1.20 m). If making the flight oneself it is simple to increase the width by adding 12in (30.5cm) wide panels.

THE HOUSE
Timber is very expensive, but to make a robust and secure house it is better not to skimp on size. Make structural members from $1\frac{1}{2}$ in square (3.8cm square) timber, and for cladding use tongued and grooved planks; preferably $\frac{5}{8}$ in (1.6 cm) thick. Make front, back and sides in separate sections, the framework to include frames for door,

41

window and pophole. Use galvanised nails. Bolting together of the finished sections is recommended, so before cladding the sections drill holes for the bolts in one mating face of the uprights only. Drilling through when the sections are put together avoids misalignment. Drill holes in base members to take screws to rawlplug the house to the base. Roofing felt deteriorates, needing eventual replacement, but there is one good system that will both insulate and provide a covering that will not need maintenance. Make and screw to the roof a framework of battens, into which can be inserted a standard thickness and width of insulation material; polystyrene is easy to cut and fit. When in position cover with corrugated PVC roofing sheets.

If a ridge roof is used, the gap along the ridge will need to be closed; this can be achieved by first applying a roll of self-adhesive sealing material, and securing by drilling along a length of plastic guttering, to fit over and screw through the PVC sheets into the roof.

FLIGHT PANELS

As for the house $1\frac{1}{2}$ in (3.8cm) square timber is recommended for making the framework and for the screening 1 in by $\frac{1}{2}$ in (2.54cm $\times$ 1.27 cm) by 19 SWG galvanised twilweld or weldmesh, 36in (1m) wide. Make panels in the standard size 6ft $\times$ 3ft (2m $\times$ 1m) and if the flight width is to be 4ft (1.20m) some in 6ft $\times$ 1ft (2m $\times$ 30cm) will be required. Having cut tops, bottoms and sides to length, next drill holes in one upright only, to take bolts for joining the panels when erecting; also drill holes in bottom members only to take screws for rawlplugging to the base. To complete the framework join with two nails at each corner; to avoid splitting the timber, drill two undersize holes in one mating surface only, marking their positions by using an offcut from the timber. To make sure that the wire mesh is not floppy on the framework, first staple one side and end only to the timber. To complete, insert staples in the other sides at an angle pointing outwards, this will tension the wire. If the frame bows slightly, ignore this as it will pull back when the frames are bolted together.

PRESERVATIVES

On no account use creosote as it is toxic, takes a long time to dry and, if deposited on the birds' feathers in any quantity, could be fatal. Cuprinol is very satisfactory, but although more expensive there is now a new improved product available. This is available in a range of colours, is no different in application, causes no damage to plants, is resin bonded, and water based, dries in a few hours, and is long lasting and non-fading. It is made by Pan-Britannic Industries Ltd under the product name of Bio Woody. For the inside of the house use a white, primer-sealer paint. This not only gives more light, but is easy to clean and further coats can be applied as required.

5   Breeding Cockatiels

When commencing breeding operations, wherever the owner lives and in whatever climate, one thing is more important than anything else: the birds *must* be in real breeding condition. This means the cocks spreading their shoulders, singing lustily, and 'drumming' on every available surface. The hens must be sleek, willing to be mated, and climbing around looking for a nest site.

Cockatiels vary enormously in their sexual activity. Some are very active, others are considerably more staid in their affairs.

The coming of spring means preparation for the breeding season. The owner of cockatiel breeding pairs will no doubt do everything possible to ensure that 'pair bonds' are formed as he or she wishes. This may mean putting the chosen pairs together in large cages for a week or perhaps two, which usually ensures that the birds will 'take' to each other. It should be remembered, however, that some birds are simply incompatible with certain other birds. Put with different partners they will settle down happily.

One thing is essential to successful breeding; remove all odd cocks and hens from colony flights where breeding is to take place, or from adjacent aviaries where birds are kept one pair to a flight. Single birds can prove extremely troublesome during the breeding season, preventing hens from getting into their boxes and breaking up somewhat tentative pair bonds by philandering cocks or flirting in the case of hens.

Breeders of show standard and new mutation cockatiels will of course be using single flights for their pairs. A comfortable size aviary for one pair of birds consists of a 3ft × 3ft × 6ft (1 × 1 × 2m) high house and a flight 3ft (1m) wide by 9 ft (3m) long by 6ft (2m) high. Senior citizens and others will appreciate the comfort and security of an entrance porch to an aviary or block of aviaries. The small extra expense is well rewarded by the ease of entrance and the prevention of birds from escaping.

Porches are particularly useful with a colony aviary. Where there are a number of birds breeding together, young ones must often be caught for sale or to remove to another aviary. To use a net in these circumstances is extremely upsetting to the breeding birds and can lead to young being crushed in the nest. It is however relatively easy to drive a few birds at a time into the entrance porch assuming that the owner has fitted a secure bolt on the inside of the porch. Young birds will fly towards an entrance, older ones are often far too clever, and when they want to get rid of their 'first round' they will often lead the way into the porch and then fly back at the last split second before the inner door closes, leaving the youngsters behind!

For those who are not concerned with show standards, or new and expensive mutations requiring a carefully controlled breeding programme over a number of years, colony breeding can be confidently recommended. A 'colony' aviary could be said to be any aviary which contains two or more pairs of cockatiels. Cockatiels are colony birds in the wild state, searching about for food and water over mainly rather arid land.

Anyone who has seen the happiness and well being of a well-adjusted colony of cockatiels will soon see how their ancestral ways persist to this day. In order to arrive at a well-adjusted colony it will be necessary to put the intended pairs, hopefully already pair-bonded, together some weeks before breeding is to start. Young pairs who have already mated together should be introduced to each other preferably during the autumn or winter months so that there is plenty of time to see if one or more are 'trouble makers'. Some perfectly good birds just do not fit into colony life and must be allowed to breed on their own. It may be that the hen is very nervous or that the cock cannot keep his eyes off hens other than his own, and is forever philandering with other cocks' mates instead of getting on with the business of breeding. Do not imagine that the above problems will be avoided simply by putting the offending pair into a single aviary. Nervous hens will still be nervous, but less so, and amorous cocks will still give the 'glad eye' to hens in the next aviary, but at least will not be able to do anything else.

Many years of breeding colony cockatiels as well as single aviary pairs has so far shown me that even if the flight is quite large and the house is large, one will start off with, for example, six pairs and end up with four pairs breeding; the others will have had to be removed for one reason or another. They may have been too wild, too shy, too nervous, or were bullies, or were too inquisitive and interfered with other birds' affairs. An ideal situation is where the house is quite big, 4ft 6in by 6ft (1½m × 2m) and the flight 6ft × 9ft (2m × 3m). This size aviary will house four pairs very comfortably, with two nest boxes in the house and two in the flight, as far apart as possible. It must be remembered that as soon as the birds start to come into breeding condition they are looking and fighting for territory, and that their nest box and surrounding space is their territory. I never put spare nest boxes in a colony aviary. The cocks will try to hold the extra territory of a spare box, and will often actively encourage their hens to leave young in the nest and go and lay more eggs in another box (a sort of avian one-upmanship!). One box per pair is enough, if the hens are desperate they will lay their eggs amongst the young in their box, and the young of one round will help to incubate the young of the next round.

Cockatiels will nest in various sizes of nest box, but very small

44

boxes are not recommended. The reason for this is that although in theory the cock sits during the day and the hen at night, when the weather is cold, and during and after hatching, the two of them are often in the box together. The risk of eggs getting squashed and tiny birds crushed is very much greater in a very small box.

The size of nest box I use is $9\frac{1}{2}$ in square by 14 in high (24 cm square by 34.5 cm high) with a 3 in (7.6 cm) diameter hole cut $1\frac{1}{2}$ in (3.8 cm) from the top. I insert a 6 in (15 cm) perch made from $\frac{1}{2}$ in (1.27 cm) doweling by pushing it through a hole bored $1\frac{1}{2}$ in (3.8 cm) below the entrance hole. About $2\frac{1}{2}$ in (6 cm) of perch should be sufficient on the inside. The wood for the box can be blockboard, but of course solid wood is preferable; $\frac{3}{4}$ in (1.9 cm) thick will give the birds some protection from cold and also heat in very hot weather. A removable lid is both safer and easier to manage than a hinged one, which can sometimes fall back just as one is trying to remove chicks.

A ladder of one sort or another is essential in cockatiel nest boxes. It encourages the adults to go in and investigate a prospective 'home' and without it baby birds cannot get out of the box if the nesting material is at the normal level. The type of ladder often fitted is a piece of weldmesh or wiremesh attached to two $\frac{3}{4}$ in (2 cm) thick pieces of wood fitted to the inside of the front of the box about 4 in (10 cm) apart and reaching from just underneath the inside perch to about 4 in (10 cm) from the bottom. The great disadvantage with this very common type of ladder is that baby birds endeavouring to get out of the nest may lose their grip or, more likely, get their claws caught in the wire and panic, falling backwards and sometimes severely damaging their legs. Baby birds have been known to die in these circumstances.

By far the safest form of ladder is a $1\frac{1}{2}$ in (3 cm) square piece of wood, with quite deep 'steps' cut in its whole length. This ladder should reach rather higher than the level of the inside perch, and it should be fitted to one front corner of the inside of the box. Because they provide endless amusement to both parents and young, who pass long hours in the box gnawing at the wood, these ladders do need frequent renewal from year to year.

If the ladder is found to be worn smooth by the gnawing of the parents it will be necessary to raise the level of the nesting material in order to make it possible for the chicks to get out of the box. No harm will be done if the chicks are carefully removed near to the time when the eldest wants to leave the nest. They should be put into a deep towel-lined bowl while more nesting material, which should be warm and dry, is put in the box to bring the level up to $1\frac{1}{2}$ in (3.8 cm) from the entrance hole. A slight concave should be made with the hand in the nesting material and the chicks can be returned.

Some apparently quite healthy cockatiels do feed their young in such a manner that the droppings are extremely wet. When the chicks are very young, leave well alone as the droppings act as a sort of 'hot-bed' set up by the chemical reaction of the excreta on the nesting material, making it warm; gardeners will recognise this term. When the chicks are older and get their feathers it is as well to take them out one at a time and free their toes of the accumulated mess which will stick like rock-hard 'bobbles' on the ends of each toe, making it very hard for them to grip the ladder in order to climb out. At this stage the worst of the wet mess in the box can usefully be removed and clean, dry and warm material put in its place.

Nesting materials vary so much that it is difficult to recommend any particular one. Wood chips are used by many people, the disadvantage being that tiny chips can be swallowed by the chicks, sometimes with disastrous results when they get stuck in their crops. The same may apply to sawdust; and there is the added risk that it may have been treated with poisonous chemicals.

Many large parrot-type birds like to nest in rotted wood. If this is provided for cockatiels it should be broken down completely to a coarse powder. Unlike most larger parrots and parakeets, they will not break it down themselves and may refuse to nest in it altogether. If it is used, care must be taken to avoid rotted wood from trees such as pines, which contains resin, and from silver birches and oak, both of which can be harmful to birds. Beech would be harmless and I have used the rotted wood of chestnuts for larger parrot-type birds.

The nesting material I prefer to use for cockatiels is Irish brown moss peat. It is clean and easy to use and the birds always take to it at once. When it is put in the nesting boxes it should be very slightly moist at the bottom of the box and finished off with a top layer of dry, finely crumbled peat; a depth of about 5 in (13 cm) is satisfactory. A little compressed pet litter on top gives extra comfort.

Many newcomers are puzzled as to when to put up nest boxes. If introduced too early, and in a cold climate, the eggs will very likely get badly chilled at some time and will not hatch; too late and the birds will rush to nest and the first eggs will not be fertile. Of the two alternatives, it is much safer in a cold climate to wait for the hen's sake until the weather is reasonable before putting up nest boxes. Egg binding is far less likely when the temperature is 60°F (15°C) or more.

To some extent one must be guided by the condition of the birds. Once they have reached the 'zenith' of health and 'breeding condition' it is best to allow cockatiels to go to nest, otherwise the hens may lay from the perch or on the floor. Both members of the pair may then go right out of condition and take a long time to return to their original peak of health.

Male cockatiels will start to show interest in breeding at ten months of age or younger in some cases. Females usually start to show interest at eleven months or younger in occasional cases.

Cocks breed well up to twelve years of age, while hens lay fewer and fewer eggs after about six years. Some older birds make very good foster parents, but not all cockatiels will act as foster parents to other cockatiels' young, and some will not even accept another bird's eggs, depositing them in the cold at the side of the box within hours of them being introduced.

Cockatiels are generally excellent and loving parents, taking great pride in their young. Many hens step aside in the box to proudly display their eggs or young. They respond so much to a word or a whistle of encouragement, and are touchingly anxious to draw their owner's attention to their progeny, whether they are newly hatched or just out of the nest box.

Unless the weather is extremely warm, young birds who have just emerged from the box should not be left on the floor of the aviary, and at this time it is also very important to ensure that any water containers have a small stepping stone in them to enable a young bird to get out. This is especially important in a colony where some breeding pairs are more advanced than others.

At a certain stage in incubation the hens will want to be able to bathe in water well up to their middles. This gives necessary humidity to the eggs; the water needs to be about 2 in (5 cm) deep.

Infertile eggs can be extremely useful as 'props' for baby birds and also as 'hot water bottles'. They are best left in place until the brood is well advanced, but embryos dead in shell should be removed.

Handling of eggs can lead to mistakes being made and fertile eggs being thrown out because the veins are not visible. I prefer to leave well alone. The incubation period can vary between 17 and 22 days, but it may be even longer in cold weather.

In cool spring weather a pinch of niger seed per bird is helpful as the hens start to lay. The seed must be fresh and very shiny. Old or broken seed is very harmful in the case of all oily seeds, because the oil turns rancid.

Cockatiels vary enormously in what they will take to feed their young, but one thing never seems to vary; one of the first items fed to a newly hatched baby bird is finely powdered cuttlefish bone. The parents clearly consider that this is the best and quickest way to introduce calcium and some other mineral elements such as salt into their young. All cockatiels should have a constant supply of *fresh* 'mineralised' grit, oyster shell grit and cuttlebone available to them at all times; and during the breeding season it is particularly important to give powdered cuttlebone to the birds, fresh every day.

Parents feeding young work extremely hard, particularly the cocks, and everything possible should be done to make life easy for them. Cockatiels, like humans, seem to have phases or 'fashions' in what they will eat, and on what they will feed their young. Many years ago it was normal practice to supply all breeding birds with

47

Large water containers, smaller containers and usefully sized catching net with appropriately padded edge.

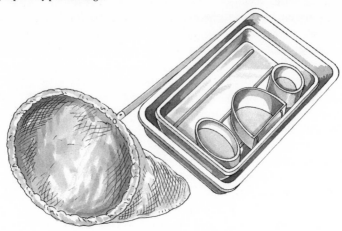

soaked seed, usually a mixture of millet and canary seed, soaked in water for twenty four hours and then rinsed and supplied twice per day. Then somebody discovered that various fungi can exist and grow on the soaked seed, so less of it was fed, and now it is almost impossible to get cockatiels to feed on that food.

One food which all cockatiels continue to like all the year round is brown bread and milk. The bread is held under water for a few seconds, then squeezed out. Some milk (boiled in hot weather) is poured over the bread, which is then squeezed out and crumbled. All cockatiels like either crumbled hard boiled egg yolk, or, perhaps more popular with them, an egg-rearing food. Many birds like one containing a little honey. These foods should be supplied fresh, twice per day. Egg foods should not be given to cockatiels except during the breeding season: it is very rich, and their livers are not designed to deal with such a food all the year round. Some cockatiels insist on feeding their young from a very early age on large quantities of dry sunflower seed. The young birds appear to grow just as fast and be just as healthy as any others and soon learn to eat a more varied diet when they get out of the nest.

All cockatiels should have a constant, fresh daily supply of green and root foods: various cabbages, lettuces, carrots and celery form the basis of their green food diet in the UK. To this can be added any wild foods, such as seeding dandelion heads and seeding hawkweed heads which are deemed to be free of poisonous sprays, petrol and diesel fumes. Chickweed, so much liked by nearly all cockatiels, may harbour the eggs of hair or threadworms (*Capillaria*), so is best avoided. From gardens in cool countries the seeding heads of forget-me-nots, calendula and wild honeysuckle flowers are greatly enjoyed by cockatiels, and do them no harm.

48

Cockatiel chicks leave the nest at between four and five weeks old, rather depending on the weather, and the last chick of a nest will often struggle out, unable to fly, at three weeks old if the weather is hot, or if it is frightened by other older nestlings peering into the nest.

Many people wish to close ring their birds. A word of caution is needed here. Before putting on a close ring *do* make very certain that the ring is sufficiently large. Check with the makers. The suffering caused in later life by a metal ring which is too small is intense; and it will probably mean a journey to a veterinarian to get the ring cut away after the bird has been anaesthetised. Some modern mutation cockatiels have such short, fat legs that the fitting of closed rings, which are quite wide, is most undesirable. When the birds are about three months of age it is usually relatively easy to fit split metal rings and the use of these rings is increasing greatly. These rings are made to order in the closed ring colour of the year and can have the owner's initials, numbers, etc., stamped on them.

Two people are required to fit the ring, one to hold the bird with one leg extended, while the other closes the ring so that the two sides just meet. These rings are generally made of aluminium, and tend to 'spring' at the last moment, resulting in a badly overlapping, tightly fitting ring. Great care must be exercised with the small pliers needed for fitting. It helps if the bird is allowed to chew on a gloved hand.

Closed rings must be fitted about the time the young bird's eyes are opening, which is usually between the ages of eight and ten days. The three biggest toes of one leg are gently pushed through the ring until it is over the end of the smallest toe. A sharpened matchstick is then inserted under the smallest toe which is eased through the ring. Young birds vary enormously in their rate of growth, even from the same nest; and some have such short fat legs that it would be most unwise to try to fit a closed ring. In these cases fit a metal split ring later. Split celluloid rings which simply unwind and spring back into place are much easier to fit, and are useful from the age of about ten weeks for identification when sorting out cocks from hens. They come in many colours.

The young cockatiels must be wormed by the age of ten weeks. From this age until they are five or six months old they need half an adult's dose. Instructions for worming are given in the chapter on hygiene (Chapter 9).

Young cockatiels can feed themselves adequately from the age of about seven weeks; some will be more forward, others take a little longer to be self-supporting. Young from the first nest are best removed from their parents at about eight weeks old to enable the cock to have a rest: he does most of the feeding once the young leave the nest.

It is most unwise to allow cockatiels to breed themselves to a standstill. Ten to twelve young should be quite sufficient for anyone, and will amply repay money laid out for top quality stock the previous year. Two nests, or at the most three, should produce the above numbers of young. It is particularly important not to allow young cockatiels to go on breeding in their first year. It can take too much of their strength and make them poor breeders during the second and successive years, which are far more important.

BREEDING RECORDS AND PEDIGREES

When breeding cockatiels it is most important to keep correct breeding records. Breeding record forms can be bought, and are excellent for those with neat handwriting. Others may prefer to make their own, with more space for information about the appearance of each bird, and its sex, etc.

Many people like to keep pedigrees of their stock, for which forms are also available, and are sometimes advertised. It is not difficult to set out a simplified version of an animal's pedigree, using ring numbers for the ancestry of the bird concerned.

6   Incubators, Incubation and Brooders

CONSIDERATIONS FOR INCUBATION

It may happen, especially with young inexperienced pairs of birds, that the eggs are left: the hen does not brood, or a young cock will not sit consistently during the days. Whatever the reason, most people will choose to make efforts to save the eggs.

The first consideration will be to find out if another pair already sitting will accept the eggs, in which case the best time to introduce the eggs is when the hen is sitting. If the eggs cannot be fostered, artificial incubation can be considered, and if one already has an incubator and previous experience, there should be no problem in hatching fertile cockatiel eggs.

Artificial incubation opens up a further interesting and exciting aspect of the hobby, but it must be borne in mind that the hardest task is hand-feeding after the eggs are hatched. This is very time-consuming and should not be undertaken unless someone can be on hand to feed the chicks at the times required, to ensure their survival.

Before purchasing an incubator there are many aspects that must be considered to avoid making a wrong decision. Associated equipment will also be required: an 'egg candler' to check if the eggs are fertile, and a 'brooder' to house the chicks and ensure that they are kept in the right environment after they are hatched.

There are many incubators available on the market, but most are of two types: still air and forced air incubators. Most will have been designed and built to hatch chicken, quail and pheasant eggs, so it is important to remember that the criteria for hatching these eggs are not the same as those of parrot and parrot-like birds.

STILL AIR INCUBATORS

There is a large range of still air incubators available and those in the small sizes are certainly the cheapest. However, they are not ideal for hatching cockatiel eggs, as natural convection, even with solid-state temperature control, does not allow for the close control and adjustment required for the ideal temperature and humidity. Moreover, most will not have automatic turning of the eggs, which will be required to be turned at least five times spread over twenty four hours.

FORCED AIR INCUBATORS

The air circulated by electrically-driven fans ensures equal

Marsh Turn-X incubator.

temperature throughout the cabinets of forced air incubators, and control of both temperature and humidity is more easily maintained. Coupled with automatic turning of the eggs, this is the recommended type of model to choose.

We use the 'Marsh Turn-X Incubator' which is shown in the photograph. It is the smallest Marsh model available but has plenty of capacity. Twenty four cockatiel eggs can be housed in the two inner rings alone. In practice I have used only the middle ring which has a capacity for up to sixteen eggs. The dome of this model is made of clear plastic, the air is fan circulated, turning is fully automatic, and the solid-state thermal control is adjustable and accurate. It is supplied with an adjustable exterior water fountain and there are a range of turning rings to suit various sizes of eggs. This particular incubator has been used each year over a period of five years, during which time there were no breakdowns or maintenance problems. It is, nevertheless, essential to clean thoroughly and disinfect at the end of each season, and apply a couple of small squirts from an aerosol can of WD-40® oil to the fan bearing, bending the small plastic tube supplied with the tin at an angle, and inserting it through a small hole in the top plastic cover, so that the oil mist is directed into the bearing. Care must be taken to ensure that the oil goes only where required, and be careful not to over-oil, or the action of the fan will spread oil over a large area. This product is available in car accessory shops and is manufactured by WD-40 Company Ltd (see list of Useful Addresses). Consistently successful hatching, not only of cockatiels but also of grass parakeets, has been achieved using this incubator.

The Marsh incubators are made in the USA by Lyon Electric Co. Inc. of San Diego, California, USA. The main distributors and service agents in the UK are Robin Haigh Incubators (see list of Useful Addresses). Robin Haigh has spent many years breeding, incubating and hand rearing a variety of birds, so that expert advice is available for the users of the equipment he supplies.

EGG CANDLERS

These can be purchased, but are very easy to make. Select a medium sized standard cardboard transport box, approximately 10 in $\times$ 8 in $\times$ 5 in (25.5 $\times$ 20 $\times$ 13 cm).

Take a 40 watt pearl electric light bulb and fit it into a bulb-holder of the type designed to fit into the top of a bottle to be used as a lampshade. The reason for this is that this type of bulb-holder includes an integral on/off switch. It is essential that heat does not build up in the egg when being viewed, so the switch allows for ease of control. For those who want to view eggs from very expensive birds, it would be prudent to include a small cooling fan in the box. At the end of the box, opposite the opening flap and 1.5 in (3.81 cm) up from the bottom and in the centre, make a hole so that the bulb-holder can be fitted closely in and secured by the screwed cap. The aim is to have the top of the bulb, when fitted, at least 2 in (5 cm) from the top of the box, to avoid overheating the egg. In the top of the box immediately above the centre of the bulb make a $\frac{3}{4}$ in (2 cm) diameter hole upon which to place the egg.

If a variety of sizes of eggs from other birds also need to be candled, a larger hole should be made, and various hole sizes to suit made in flat pieces of rubber to be placed over the top of the hole. Wire up with a suitable length of cable to reach the mains supply and the box is ready for use.

BROODERS

The brooder must be a flexible piece of equipment as it has to maintain a high, reasonably accurate temperature for chicks that have just been hatched. As the temperature has to be progressively reduced, the control must be easy to handle. The chicks will need regular removal for feeding, so access also needs to be easy. There is nothing more exasperating than having to unfasten and remove covers. As the chicks grow, they will at times tend to move away from the heat source, although it will still need to be available, so provision should be made for them to be able to move from and to the heat. As their eyes open they will need to look around, so a completely enclosed container is not ideal. I also consider that it is better to have the heat directed from above rather than below, as it is a much more natural condition. Finally, cleanliness and hygienic conditions are most important for the good health of the chicks.

There are a number of purpose-built brooders advertised; many in satisfactory use, but at the time of writing it was considered that none on offer would fulfil all the requirements envisaged. The subject of brooders was discussed with Rosemary Low, and she explained how to make the type of brooder that she was finding very satisfactory at that time. I therefore decided to make something on similar lines that would satisfy my requirements. So I set to and produced the equipment, which I found to be ideal to use. There are two versions. The cost of the first is minimal, and the second is a modification of the first, but with a thermostat. This was found necessary for the area in which we live, as on very cold mornings the temperature in the brooder dropped when everyone in the district switched on their electrical appliances at breakfast time.

The photograph shows the original control board with the thermostat that was added.

Control panel for home made brooder.

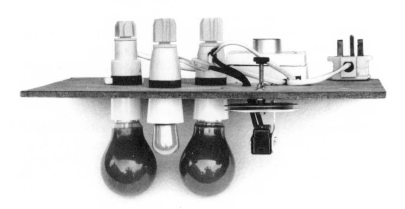

Making The Brooder
The basic idea is to have a separate control board made from a rectangular piece of plywood on which is mounted the electrical equipment, complete with a plug for connecting to the main electrical supply. The control board is then placed across the end of a

cardboard box. The size can be flexible provided the board overlaps on three sides.

Boxes are easily obtained from supermarkets. Remember, cleanliness is vital, so choose a clean box which is as thick as possible, preferably made from smooth cardboard. The advantage of using these boxes is that they can be discarded and replaced frequently. To make the board, a piece of $\frac{1}{4}$ in (0.63 cm) thick plywood 15 in × 10 in (38 × 25 cm) is required. Draw two lines along the middle of both length and breadth to find the centre. Drill or cut two central holes 1$\frac{1}{4}$ in (3 cm) in diameter, 4 in (10 cm) apart on the lengthwise line, i.e. 2 in (5 cm) each side of the centre.

Two sockets to take electric light bulbs should then be fitted into these holes and secured by their screwed caps. Allowing sufficient room for wiring up, place a standard dimmer switch to the side and rear of the light fittings and firmly bolt to the board. Read the instructions supplied with the dimmer switch and wire up, including a plug for connection to the mains electricity.

Two 40 watt electric light bulbs coloured dark red should be used. The reason is twofold: if one bulb fails there will still be some warmth, and dark bulbs are gentle on the eyesight of the chicks. A thermometer should be placed alongside the chicks in whatever receptacle that they are housed in; preferably one of the long narrow types, so that it can be easily read when protruding from the covering. When the brooder is first used, care and time will need to be spent turning the dimmer switch and checking to reach the required temperature. The photograph shows the control board resting on top of a box. The top of the box is open and the front has been cut away. Twilweld has been loosely fitted by bending around the open areas. For very young chicks it does not have to fit very firmly, and needs to be easily removable for access. The advantages of using the box are that access is easy, chicks can be seen, and with the thermometer left in position the temperature can be readily checked. As the chicks grow they can not only see out and around, but can move freely to and from the warm area.

If you decide from the onset to make a control board with a thermostat to regulate the temperature, a dimmer switch is not necessary. The best thermostat to use is the ether-capsule type. These can be found in the shops selling aquarium equipment, but need to be checked carefully for suitability. The one shown in the photograph was made in the USA by Marsh-Lyon, model T.S.1 Wafer Thermostat Unit, and this variety can be obtained from Robin Haigh Incubators (see list of Useful Addresses).

Fitting the thermostat to the board is simple. Remove the capsule by unscrewing the control rod by the knob. Drill two holes to match the centres of the holes in the bracket, and bolt it in position on the underside, 2 in from the eight bulbs. Then drill a further hole to give

55

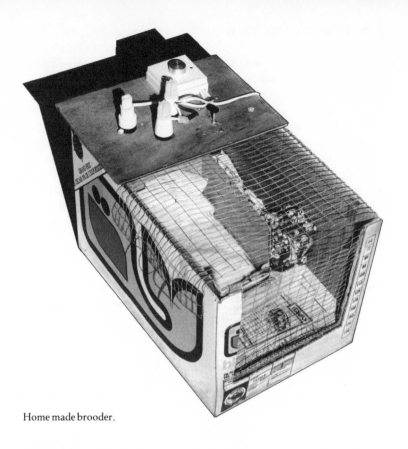

Home made brooder.

correct alignment for the control rod to be fitted through the capsule in position underneath. A further hole is needed to allow the electrical wires to be fed from the bottom to the top of the board.

The first time the thermostat was fitted to the board we immediately noticed how the lights flashed on and off in response to the operation of the micro-switch. This would be very disturbing to the chicks, so a third socket and bulb was added. The bulb in this case is small; a pygmy 15 watt, coloured red. The wiring was then arranged so that the control of the temperature only operated through this small bulb.

The thermostat is set by turning the knob, so that the micro-switch operates in accordance with the temperature required on the thermometer in the box below.

USING THE INCUBATOR
Having obtained an incubator, the first thing to do is to read carefully the instruction book. It is surprising how many people are too anxious to start operating their new equipment before fully understanding how it will work.

SITING THE INCUBATOR

A careful choice of where the incubator should be positioned must be made. It should not be placed where it could be affected by fluctuating heat or cold conditions: that is, not in direct sunlight or draughts. Ideally it should be in a steady temperature of 70°F (20°C), but this is not critical. A place where the surrounding temperature will be fairly even will suffice, but be careful not to place it where children or animals could upset it. A sheet of foam rubber underneath will reduce the hum from a fan.

Use a table that is large enough to accommodate any parts needed to be removed for inspection or removal of the eggs, and containers, record cards, pad and pen. Always remember the importance of cleanliness and hygiene as newly-hatched chicks can so easily pick up infections.

PREPARING FOR OPERATION

This is a most critical time, for it is vital that any equipment is working correctly, in all aspects, over a short period before any eggs are introduced. When first setting up, the incubator must be clean. If it has been used previously, it should first be cleaned with a mild soap, ammonia and water, or a commercial product advertised for this purpose; do not use harsh detergents. Having set it up and plugged it in, the first check should be to see that the eggs will turn correctly, with the automatic turning device operating. On my 'Marsh Turn-X' the second row of the turning ring is used. Taking a useless egg, mark one side in the centre with an 'X' and the opposite side with an 'O'. (If a good egg is to be used, mark with a felt pen to avoid damage.) Place on the turning ring, small end towards the centre, 'X' uppermost. Operate the automatic turner by the override button and adjust the instructions to give a 180° turn. The mechanism reverses the turn after one hour; a full 180° turn is not critical. I do not fill the water fountain at this stage, but run the incubator for twenty four hours to allow the temperature to build up and become stable, ready for final adjustments. It is sensible to allow a total of forty eight hours for setting up and adjustments before any eggs are set for incubation.

HUMIDITY

To ensure that disaster does not strike at hatching time, a high percentage of humidity in the incubator must be avoided. Good hatching during incubation with my cockatiels has been achieved with humidity at around 50 per cent. As the normal humidity outside the incubator is usually well above this figure, the amount of water placed inside the incubator needs to be minimal. Many people, when first starting, make the mistake of thinking that plenty of space for water means that a lot should be put in to give the percentage of

57

humidity required. It is far better to add a little than have to syphon out a lot. I prefer to use distilled water, and before filling the Marsh Turn-X water bottle, screw up the adjusting screw so that only two threads show above the screw. When carefully placed in position, the water should only fill half the first compartment in the base. Humidity is checked by attaching a wick to the horizontally-mounted thermometer. The end of the wick is placed in the water. When all the wick is wet, check the thermometer reading. 84°F (21°C) is 50 per cent humidity. If adjustment is needed, add or take away a very little water at a time. Accuracy using the wick does not last for very long; once satisfied that humidity is around 50 per cent it is best not to take any more readings, as it should not be necessary. To obtain the relative percentage of humidity, reference must be made to a chart, after noting the reading on the wet bulb thermometer.

WITH AN INCUBATION TEMPERATURE OF 99.5°F (37.5°C) (DRY BULB READING)	
WET BULB THERMOMETER READING	HUMIDITY
82°F (27.7°C)	46%
83°F (28.3°C)	48%
84°F (28.8°C)	50%
85°F (29.3°C)	53%
86°F (30.0°C)	56%
87°F (30.5°C)	59%
88°F (31.1°C)	62%
89°F (31.6°C)	65%
90°F (32.2°C)	68%
91°F (32.8°C)	70%

Dry is below 45 per cent; normal is 50 per cent; humid is above 55 per cent. Owing to the position and small size of the thermometers, they are not always easy to read. I find it easier to read the percentage directly from a dial type humidity gauge; it is an inexpensive alternative, sits flat on the turning ring, and is accurate to within ± 5 per cent. With all humidity gauges, accuracy is only maintained a short time and after four weeks should be recalibrated to the manufacturer's instructions. Normal gauges can be obtained from the incubator supplier, or a dual purpose gauge indicating both temperature and relative humidity (reference No. T.9108/1) can be obtained from Casella Ltd (see list of Useful Addresses).

TEMPERATURE
Adjustments to the thermostat can now be made to obtain the constant heat required for incubation. The solid-state temperature control on the Marsh Turn-X is very accurate to ± 0.1°F (0.06°C)

and adjustment is by means of a knurled rod which extends through the dome. It is advisable to have an accurate spare thermometer, a mercury-filled type reading with increments of 1°F (0.6°C). If the incubator is likely to be in regular use, I would recommend obtaining a digital reading electronic thermometer. The readings are made quickly, are clearly shown and accurate to ±1°F (±0.6°C). Debate continues on the best temperature to use, ranging from 98.5°F (36.9°C) to 100°F (37.8°C). Having had success with 99.5°F (37.5°C), I recommend this as the temperature to use. Care and time must be taken to adjust the thermostat so that this temperature is accurate and constant. It always takes a long time when first using an incubator and, once satisfied, let it run for twenty four hours before putting in the eggs to commence incubation.

INCUBATING
The eggs to be placed in an incubator must first be examined for cleanliness, and any sign of damage. Eggs that are dirty must not be washed, as any bacteria that may be present could permeate the porous shell. It is forbidden by law in the UK to wash commercially-produced poultry eggs. They do not have to be sparkling clean but any deposits on the shell should be gently removed using fine sandpaper or wire wool. Eggs badly cracked should be discarded, but a small dent could be covered with clear nail varnish, or the New Skin® product obtainable from the chemist.

Cold eggs must not be placed in the incubator, but should slowly and carefully be warmed up to 80° to 90°F (26.8° to 32.3°C), over a period of a few hours. An airing cupboard can be a good place, but first make sure it is not too hot. The time needed to hatch cockatiel eggs can vary from 18 to 22 days. In hot weather out of doors it can often be the former.

For incubation assume 21 days, and prepare a chart in readiness, showing the date, estimated time of hatching, and number of eggs; list the number of days, leaving space alongside each day to record checks of temperature, humidity, candling, etc. Place the eggs in the incubator, making sure the automatic turning device is connected. Having opened the incubator, the temperature will fall, and the cooler eggs might also contribute to a small drop, but leave alone for some hours and it should stabilise very quickly. Thereafter check daily, filling in the chart accordingly. The eggs will be tolerant to minor differences so only adjust if necessary. Watch the water bottle and refill it when empty, being careful not to flood the incubator when doing this. It is best to practise beforehand. The eggs should be candled to check for fertility. Many people check after only a few days, but I recommend at ten days as one has to be experienced at looking through the eggs to reach the right conclusions. A spidery web of small veins, a small blob and an air gap filling about one quarter of the large end indicates fertility and progress, but if the egg appears to be clear do not yet discard it. Be sure to handle the egg with clean hands and remember not to overheat by taking too long to view when it has been placed over the light. Re-check a few days later to make a final decision. Turning of the eggs should be halted three days before hatching is due, and the amount of water increased to give 70+ per cent humidity as this helps to make the shell more suitable for pipping.

When pipping occurs, the time taken for the chick to emerge can vary greatly. Some chicks can be out quickly, others could take up to 48 hours, so be patient. It is rare that cockatiels have difficulty in getting out of the egg, but if, after 36 hours, there appears to be a problem and pipping is not continuing, the egg could be removed. Look for the airgap and gently remove a small part of the shell from this area, using a sharp sterilised instrument, a needle or tip of a penknife. Examine the membrane; veins showing a red pattern of blood means hatching is not yet due. In this case immediately cap with a cleaned part of a hen's egg and return to the incubator. Re-examine in twelve hours; if the vascular pattern has receded, the chick is ready to come out of the shell. Examine the membrane and if it is very tough, brush gently with warm boiled water to moisten. It may be necessary to carefully remove the membrane to release the chick. In such difficult hatching circumstances, make sure the beak is first freed from the membrane and give the chick a drop of warmed boiled water and glucose; as much as will go on the tip of a kitchen knife to half a teaspoon of water. Once chicks are hatched they do not require feeding immediately. Leave them in the incubator for four to six hours for their fluff to dry out before transferring them to the brooder for hand feeding.

7   Hand-rearing

From day one to day four or five is probably the most critical and difficult in the whole life of an incubator-hatched cockatiel. The brooder temperature should be 99°F (37°C) at this stage. The chick will be using up the remaining contents of the egg sac for the first 24 hours but, nevertheless, must be given nourishment.

It is not easy to get the beak of such a tiny chick open without damage; every bit of equipment suddenly appears enormous, and thick! What is really needed is a sharpened matchstick, but whatever is used it must be very slightly warm. Once the chick's mouth has been opened, and it has swallowed some liquid, the act of feeding will be welcomed and with a touch of the beak with a tiny warm spoon it will probably open its beak quite readily.

The very first 'food' is best confined to a tiny quantity of pure yoghourt; as much as will go on the end of a sharp pointed kitchen knife's tip, mixed with one large drop of boiled luke warm water, with a knife's tip full of pulverised cuttlefish bone. Be sure that the cuttlebone is very white and clean, because brown tinted will not do for a tiny baby bird. The above mixture should be stirred together and two tiny drops put in the baby's open mouth. It does help if two people do this first 'feed', one to open the beak, the other to drip the mixture on to the baby's tongue. If the baby seems weak, a knife's tip of glucose could be added to the mixture with advantage, and more boiled water will need to be added to make the mixture very runny.

In their book *Parrot Production* John and Pat Stoodley point out that yoghourt contains Vitamin K, which is very necessary for incubator-hatched chicks, to assist in blood clotting. Baby cockatiel chicks do not seem to tolerate yoghourt particularly well, but I have found that by giving only tiny quantities, mixed with the other items mentioned, once per day for the first three days only, the problem of starting the baby off on its hand-feeding programme is made easier. Some people find that this first feed is achieved better with a small paint brush. It does not really matter what is used so long as the baby gets the nourishment.

Two hours after the introduction of the yoghourt mixture, the next feed can be one part Milupa® infant food, Milupa Autumn Fruit Harvest, and one part Wysoy® baby food, mixed with warm boiled water to an extremely thin 'soup', so that it is diluted to approximately 10 per cent only of solids. From day one to day four the chicks are better on food consisting of this very thin mixture of solids and boiled water. For the first four days the feeds must be every two hours, round the clock, except for four hours sleep at night. The temperature of the brooder should be kept at 98-99°F (37°C).

A weak chick is best left in the incubator for the first day and night, and fed from there; but a strong one can be transferred to a brooder four to six hours after hatching and put in a very small tissue lined container, with its head propped up against the tissues. I have sometimes put chicks of this age in a small, rather flat teacup, well-lined of course, and this has in turn been placed in a slightly larger container, which will be getting nicely impregnated with warmth, ready for the next transfer of the chick or chicks in a few days time. Tissues need to be replaced every feeding time to keep the chicks as clean as possible. I have known them to cry like human babies when they were on soiled tissues!

If the chicks appear very hungry before each two hours is up, the solids can be increased very slightly – it should be a gradual process.

HAND-FEEDING FROM FOUR DAYS OLD ONWARDS

There are as many ways of bringing up cockatiel chicks are there are of rearing human babies. Someone once brought some up on porridge, others use all kinds of human baby foods. As with all other aspects of cockatiel management, one is learning something new every day; old methods are discarded and new ones tried.

I have spent more hours than I care to count endeavouring to see what parent cockatiels feed to newly-hatched chicks. It appears to be a feed of cuttlefish bone powder and cockatiel saliva, no doubt a powerful combination of chemicals designed by nature to set the baby bird firmly on a healthy route to its future life. Next to be fed seems to be tiny quantities of hard-boiled egg, plus celery and carrot juice, and such delicacies as dandelion, chickweed or sowthistle seeds, if available. Bread and milk comes later, with commercially produced rearing foods, and well-ground kernels of dry sunflower seeds and later still, in some cases, soaked seeds. What is noticeable is that the more experienced parents give quite a wide assortment of foods to their young from a very early age.

Cockatiels are not the easiest of birds to hand-rear: the pumping action with which parents force food down the throats of their young is impossible for us humans to simulate.

Another problem with feeding young cockatiels is getting the right temperature for the food. I always try every spoonful either against my lips or the back of my hand, and if the food feels just comfortable to the lips, it should be the right temperature. If the food is too hot, the birds will suffer scalded throats, and the risk of candidiasis later on, and if it is too cold they will refuse to eat.

I use a tiny spoon with bent edges at first but, as soon as possible, I get the young ones used to a very small, flat coffee spoon. This will not hurt the side of their growing beaks, which a bent one will do after a while. I feed first one side of the beak and then the other, so that the beak is not damaged as it grows. The birds soon learn this routine.

Warmth is the first priority for very young birds, and it is much easier to bring up two or more chicks as they help to keep each other warm. Assuming the birds to be reared are between four and ten days old, put them into a box lined with soft towelling, with tissues on top, which must be changed of course every time the birds are fed. Put the box into a brooder, and for the first ten days of the young ones' lives keep the temperature at between 95 and 99°F (35-37°C). Sometimes the babies will shiver, and other times they will pant, so be prepared to vary the temperature a little to suit them . From ten to fourteen days old the heat can start to go down, but only by a degree or two a day. It is much better to keep the chicks comfortable than to force the temperature down too quickly.

The aim should be to try to bring down the heat gradually to about 70°F (20°C) by weaning time, which usually starts at about three weeks old. Most very young cockatiels like a light covering of some material such as towelling, which seems to give them comfort and security, especially at night.

Five-day-old cockatiel chicks can manage quite well with a last feed at about 12.30 am and a first feed about 6.30 am. They are best fed every three hours from five days to nine or ten days, then every four hours, bringing the feeding down gradually to four times a day, then three times a day by the time they are three weeks old.

By the age of three weeks the young birds will begin to think about picking up odd bits of food. It is a good idea at this stage to give them a tiny well-washed twig from a hazel or apple tree to chew as this teaches them to use their beaks for themselves. Spray millet is also very good for this purpose, but it must be scalded in boiling water first, to kill off any germs. Cockatiels weighing about $\frac{1}{4}$ oz (7 g) at four days old may be expected to weigh up to around $2\frac{1}{2}$ oz (70 g) at five to six weeks old.

As with the younger chicks it is most important to prepare the food to the right consistency. From four to ten days of age the diet can consist of approximately 30 per cent solids, then after ten days it can be gradually increased to 40 then 50 per cent solids. The temptation to fill up little crops must be avoided, and absolute cleanliness is of very great importance. I often change the tissues between meals. The chicks themselves need to be kept washed and dried, especially the area around the beak, which gets caked rock hard with food if it is not cleaned, and can hurt the young birds.

At four to five days old the chicks should be given, once only, as much grit as will go on the tip of a pointed kitchen knife, and the same amount of cuttlefish bone; both must be totally pulverised. The quantities are per bird. At one week old cuttlefish bone should

63

be given once daily, and grit every two to three days. Both can be mixed into the first feed of the day when the chicks are very hungry.

From six days to about twelve or fourteen days a tiny quantity (say, one quarter of a coffee spoon per two birds) of Cow and Gate® beef and bone broth for babies should be given, once per day only. It is a good bone builder but needs to be carefully watched as it can cause the bird's skin to turn bright pink, which normally indicates too much protein in the diet. If this happens, stop the broth for a day to two and cease giving it altogether when the birds are two weeks old. Beef and bone broth is a baby food for human babies, and must be kept very cool and used within three days of opening.

The basic rearing food for cockatiels from four days old onwards is the following mixture, which is *not* cooked, but should be mixed with hot boiled water, and the container should be stood in hot water for one minute to allow the food to swell.

Put two parts of Prewett's® oatbran and oatgerm (from health food shops) with one part of Milupa® infant food autumn fruit harvest, and one part of Wysoy® powder (a baby food). To this could be added once or twice per day one part of any good egg-rearing food for birds. This mixture must be mixed to the required consistency for the age of birds.

Certain constituents of human baby foods must be watched carefully. Cockatiel babies cannot tolerate much milk, hence the reason for including that excellent rearing food for human babies, Wysoy®. This is a food especially prepared for human babies who cannot tolerate cow's milk. Baby cockatiels are also very sensitive to any form of protein, from whatever source. If their skin turns bright pink or, later, dark red to purple due to too much protein they will not last long unless the food is altered or possibly more heat is given.

As has been stressed before, cockatiels, like other birds, are individuals and some can tolerate one particular food while others cannot. Too much protein is a major source of trouble and for this reason the approximate protein content of the chief foods used is given below.

In every 100 g of Prewett's® oatbran and oatgerm there are 16.3 g of protein; Wysoy® has 16 g, Milupa® autumn fruit harvest has 12 g, and Cow and Gate® beef and bone broth has 4.7 g. The protein content of egg-rearing foods for birds varies so it cannot be given. It may be helpful to point out here that one slightly heaped teaspoon of either oatbran and oatgerm, Milupa® food or Wysoy® equals 10 g.

From seven days onwards sunflower kernels (from health food shops) can be added to the basic diet at least once per day, and more as the birds grow. They are best ground up in a coffee grinder or pulverised in some way, then put through a sieve to exclude the inner skin. They are greatly enjoyed by the baby birds, and can be added in the proportion of one part to the other basic foods.

This is an age when grated, then pulverised raw carrot, celery and the juice from raw cabbage stalk can be added to the food in the proportion of about one sixteenth part of the food, once or twice per day. Baby birds appreciate the flavour of fresh vegetables very much. They also enjoy a drop or two of warm boiled water at the end of each meal when their food is made with increased solids percentage.

Every bird is an individual; some are easy to rear, some difficult. Perhaps only one rule should be always kept in mind: do not overfeed. Having said this, some chicks really do need more than others, and it is not uncommon in a group for a strong one to feed a weaker one and for this reason it will be terribly anxious to get all it possibly can. If this is the case, the strong one should be allowed all it wants, since it will be giving away a lot of its nourishment.

Sometimes chicks will keep swallowing air with their food. All of them do this to some extent, just like human babies. The remedy is simple, once half way through the meal, and once at the end of the meal take the neck of the baby bird between the first finger and thumb and very gently press *downward*; this keeps the food in place and, hopefully expels any air.

A crop which is blown up with food and fluids which the chick cannot assimilate is all too common with hand-reared birds, and some parent-reared birds also suffer from this condition. This is known as impacted crop. In parent-reared birds the problem could be cold weather or, if sawdust is used in the nest box, a chip of wood could be stuck in the chick's throat.

With hand-reared birds the most likely reasons for impacted crop are either too low a temperature, causing the digestive system to slow down (this will produce a build-up of foods and fluids); or a sharp piece of grit stuck in the chick's throat or crop. In either case the skin of the chick can start to go pink, then red and finally purple. If this is the case, it must be helped immediately. Hold it almost upside down and very gently squeeze the crop downwards towards the beak for one or two seconds, to make it get rid of its food; return it to upright to 'rest' then repeat if necessary. Do not try to remove any firm residue from the base of the crop: keep the bird very warm and give it some sips of boiled lukewarm water for its comfort.

Having cleared the crop, put half a teaspoonful of black treacle (molasses) in one teaspoon of boiling water and dissolve. When this is comfortable to human lips, feed this mixture to the baby bird. If it is between four and seven days old, two to three beakfuls should be sufficient. If the bird is older give four to five mouthfuls; massage the crop gently and keep the bird very warm. Do not give ordinary feeds until the chick is obviously better. With some chicks it may be necessary to repeat the treatment with molasses at intervals.

Chicks who have been forced to expel undigested food by the

65

above method should be kept in a temperature of anything between 90 and 99°F (34-37°C) for a few hours while they recover. A chick of ten days of age should be placed in a position where it can get slightly away from such heat if it wishes. After this treatment it is a good idea to start the chick off on a 'light' diet of the Milupa® food mentioned above; one part Milupa® autumn fruit harvest to one sixteenth part of glucose, mixed with warm boiled water to a very runny consistency, giving about 10% solids for the first feed and increasing solids gradually.

It should always be remembered that a chick who will persist in dropping its head is more likely to suffer from digestive problems. I add glucose at least once per day to the feeds of chicks who are not as strong as I would wish, and have found the little extra energy it gives most helpful to them.

With parent-fed chicks people often blame their cockatiels for 'crushing' their young. What often happens is that when the weather and the nest box are cold, and a chick does not digest its food, it does not beg for food when the parents come to feed the brood. It gets weak and cannot move quickly, so it is accidentally crushed by the parents.

Hand-reared cockatiels should be allowed to 'explore' and move around a little from the age of fourteen days onwards. This is especially important with a chick which is being reared on its own. It should be in a position where it can see and hear plenty of action, otherwise as it grows it will become disorientated, depressed, and then ill.

I use disposable cardboard boxes for 'brooders'; the brooder unit is all contained in the wooden top which is placed over a new box for each batch of chicks. At the age of sixteen days onwards they are put in a box within a box. Two sections are cut from one end of each box and some small mesh wire or twilweld is wedged across this opening between the two boxes, to form a 'window'. The back part of the box is kept at the required temperature by the brooder unit, and a small area in front of the window is arranged with a paper flooring, which must be changed at least twice per day. On this floor is placed sand or well-sieved fine grit, seeds such as small millets and well-crushed and sieved canary seed. To this can be added a little egg-rearing food once a day. Tiny bits of pulverised greens and carrots spread around, plus pulverised cuttlefish bone, will all encourage the young birds to start endeavouring to pick up food. A hazel twig and spray millet will certainly give them the urge to start using their beaks.

At three to four weeks old the young birds should be nicely feathered and housed in a single breeder cage, covered at night. A good temperature at this age would be 70°F (20°C). They will need a piece of cuttlebone wedged between the wires to learn to grind it for themselves, plus the fine grit. Greens at this age can be chopped, carrots and celery grated, but at the same time pieces of all the above can be wedged between the wires to teach them what they will get in the future.

The young birds will need feeding less and less often from four weeks to five weeks old, and at six weeks they should be able to manage for themselves. Up to this age I always try to get them to take a feed last thing at night; it is very good for them.

Although the majority of hand-reared cockatiels become delightful, tame and intelligent pets, there is no reason why strong hand-reared birds should not be acclimatised to outdoor avaries. They make excellent breeding birds, steady and loving towards their young, and touchingly proud of them.

8　Nutrition and Feeding

The main constituents of food taken by cockatiels are seeds, bread and milk, egg-rearing foods, green foods and root vegetables. To these must be added, all the time, cuttlefish bone, mineralised grits and oystershell grit. Cockatiels are exceedingly fond of various tree branches, bark and unopened leaf buds. In Great Britain they will greatly benefit from hazelnut, beech, apple and willow. Little is known of the chemical make-up of these various branches which are so avidly devoured by cockatiels used to them, except to say that it is known that willow bark contains a form of salicylic acid, similar to aspirin. Possibly also the leaf buds the birds so much enjoy contain a proportion of insect life, which provides them with extra protein.

Until recent times aviculturists have had to rely on the data available from trials made in various parts of the world for the poultry industry, which is vast and powerful, especially in the USA and Great Britain. The industry and its various suppliers have no doubt been instrumental in aiding various universities and research establishments to carry out meticulous trials on the relative merits of various foods, and compounds of foods, usually for the purpose of producing better egg layers, faster growers, larger table poultry, smaller table poultry, etc., etc. Of course this has all been studied and noted over the years, but it has always been necessary to weigh up the value of information very carefully when it is translated into foods for aviary and caged birds. The marketers of seed suitable for caged birds have no doubt also conducted their own trials for many years in order to arrive at the best balance of seeds or rearing mixes for the benefit of pet owners and breeders who are newcomers.

Owners of aviaries with large numbers of birds are in a different position; they must know what to order from the seed merchant who may or may not have experience of the type of bird for which the food is being bought.

Fortunately some trials and studies have taken place in recent years in the USA and other places regarding food values for cockatiels. G.R. Grau, Department of Avian Sciences, University of California, Davis, wrote in *Cage and Aviary Birds* 27 April 1985 of a psittacine research project of the Department into nutrition, physiology and management of a flock of 220 cockatiels and 50 orange winged Amazon parrots. He wrote specifically of the value of sunflower seeds. Another contributor to *Cage and Aviary Birds*, during 1986, was J. Vredenbregt from the Netherlands, who gave most valuable information on the protein content of various seeds. Articles like these and much other valuable information regarding the nutrition of parrot-type birds is now becoming increasingly available to the owner and breeder of cockatiels.

In its wild state the cockatiel thrives largely on seeds in various stages of maturation plus, no doubt, what fresh green shoots it can find on trees and near rivers. The diet of the wild cockatiel is described both in Dr Lendon's revised edition of Caley's well known book *Australian Parrots in Field and Aviary,* and in Forshaw's *Parrots of Australia.* However, this does not mean to suggest that nature should not be improved upon. The modern mutation cockatiel is far removed from its wild ancestor and needs all the nutritional help that science can devise, especially when rearing its young; just as modern mankind needs somewhat refined foods for his digestion.

Some of the most important constituents of the foods given to cockatiels are listed below.

CARBOHYDRATES
These include sugar and starch, and are important sources of warmth and energy. Canary seed and millet and oats contain 50 per cent or over of carbohydrate, sunflower seed well under 50 per cent. Rape seed, hemp, niger and linseed are all, very approximately, 20 per cent carbohydrate.

FATS AND OILS
These create a reserve of stored energy and also give a heat insulation, very valuable in cold weather. Arnell and Keymer in their book *Bird Diseases,* state that an excessively high level of fat in the diet slows the emptying of the stomach and consequently the digestion of all food, interfering with the utilisation of other vital nourishment.

Canary seed, millets and oats all contain well under 10 per cent of fats, but sunflower, hemp, niger and linseed all contain between 30 per cent and nearly 50 per cent fats and oils. Obviously sunflower seed varies enormously in its oil content, according to the type and the purpose for which it was grown; some kinds, grown especially for their oil content, would be unsuitable as food for birds.

PROTEINS
These may be considered the most important building blocks of which birds are composed. Without sufficient protein to form a good body, the bird will not be a good specimen. In the body of a bird there are approximately 20 kinds of protein, of which the principal component is amino acid. Some of these amino acids are manufactured by the bird within its body; but others have to come into the bird by means of its food. Those which are contained in the food are known as essential amino acids; they cannot be made by the

bird and must, therefore, be supplied. Lack of some of these amino acids can cause various defects in the body such as twisted tongue formation, twisted feathers, slow growth, slow feather growth, and lack of feather pigment so that in some parrots for example, feathers which should be green turn yellow in small patches. The amino acids most essential to cockatiels are listed below.

ARGININE
Present in feathers.

ISOLEUCINE
Deficiency causes distortions of the tongue.

LEUCINE
Deficiency can cause deformities in the tongue and also feathers.

TYROSINE
This amino acid is needed, as is iodine, for the good health of the thyroid gland. It is involved in the manufacture of melanin, which gives colour to feathers. An albino cockatiel is almost totally lacking in the colour pigment melanin, while a normal cockatiel with its grey colouring has a large quantity of melanin in its feathers.

PHENYLALANINE
This could be perhaps called a twin of tyrosine; to some extent these amino acids can do duty for each other.

TRYPTOPHAN
This has been linked with nicotinic acid, a member of the B complex of vitamins. It and niacin, another B complex vitamin, are involved in the correct metabolism of the body: in other words, the correct digestion and use of food by the bird.

THREONINE AND VALINE
These 'essential amino acids' are both present in all the seeds mentioned above. At the time of writing, no special research appears to have been carried out on these two amino acids.

Perhaps the three most important amino acids of all are the following:

LYSINE
Lack of sufficient lysine causes bad feather formation and lack of pigment (colour) in the feathers.

METHIONINE AND CYSTINE

To some extent these can replace each other. They are perhaps the most important of all the amino acids. Both contain sulphur. Lack of methionine causes bad feather formation and slow growth of feathers in young birds. Sunflower seed, millet, niger and oats all contain the above amino acids. Hemp contains no cystine and no tyrosine. Canary seed contains no cystine.

One excellent source of amino acids is milk, hence the value of that old-fashioned rearing food, bread and milk. There may be times, such as breeding and moulting, and for young growing stock, when an additive containing the above essential amino acids may be advisable; it rather depends on the quality and variety of the seeds and other foods being given. Always remember, however, that too much protein puts a considerable strain on the kidneys.

VITAMINS

The next important components of the cockatiel's diet are the vitamins. These are complicated groups of chemicals, of which the more well known (referred to by their original names) are vitamins A, B, C, etc. As the groups grew larger and more were discovered, some were found to inter-relate with each other, for example biotin, B and H, and so those writing about them have tended to refer to them by name. Cockatiels fed a wide variety of seeds, greens and roots as well as bread and milk and rearing foods are not likely to need a further supply of artificially manufactured vitamins, but it must be remembered that this does not apply to vitamin D3, the 'sunshine' vitamin. The addition of this vitamin to the diet two or three times in the period before breeding in areas of the world where there is not an abundance of sunshine, can make all the difference to breeding hens. The following is not a full list, but serves to show where these important components of food may be found.

VITAMIN A (RETINOL)

Essential for growth, healthy skin and good vision, it can be stored in the liver. Deficiency allows disease to get a hold on the bird. Carotene, contained in plants and some roots is the substance from which the body of the bird can make vitamin A. Good sources of vitamin A are dandelion, chicory, lettuce, spinach, brussel sprouts, carrots, bread, eggs, milk, vitaminised rearing foods and sunflower seeds and, of course, cod liver oil.

The best known of the complex B group are the following.

B1 (THIAMINE)

Essential to life, vitamin B1 is involved in the metabolism of carbohydrates and it is contained in various cereal grains. Its absence would cause severe nervous problems and death.

B2 (RIBOFLAVIN)
This is responsible amongst other things for the normal functioning of the cells, and is contained in yeast, milk and most green foods and sunflower seeds. Lack of B2 is responsible for poor hatching of eggs.

B6 (PYRIDOXINE)
Vitamin B6 is used by birds in the metabolism of proteins and fat. It is contained in many foods given to birds, particularly rearing foods.

B12 (CYANO-COBALAMIN)
This is involved with the metabolism of foods and chemicals in the body. Lack of this vitamin is shown by poor appetite, hence poor growth rate, poor feathering, and reduced hatching rates. There is likely to be a lack of the vitamin if the gut bacteria are killed off by excessive doses of antibacterial drugs. It is contained in milk products and yeast, included in various rearing foods, and is also used as a tonic. It interacts with the amino acid methionine, which is important in the production of good feathering.

PANTOTHENIC ACID (B5), RELATED TO B2
Involved in the metabolism of foods, carbohydrates, fats, and proteins, B5 is necessary for the formation of acetylcholine, which is vital for various functions connected with the nervous system. The bird's requirement may be dependent on the amount of vitamin B12 in the diet. Best sources for cockatiels are yeast, also rearing foods. Wheat and oats supply this vitamin and it is also contained in sunflower seeds. It is perhaps B5 that produces the alleged muscle relaxant in the above seeds. Certainly cockatiels are extremely fond of sunflower seeds.

NICOTINIC ACID AND NIACIN
These are related substances which are involved in the work of metabolism in the bird's body. Niacin is found in sunflower seeds and is also contained in dandelion, lettuce, bread, a little in oats, and in milk, eggs and rearing foods.

BIOTIN
Sometimes put under the *B complex* heading, sometimes called vitamin H, biotin is valuable in helping the hatching rate of birds and in preventing leg deformities. It is found in yeast, and is included in rearing foods.

FOLIC ACID
Part of the *B complex*, folic acid helps in the production of some proteins in the body, and is found in yeast, green leaves, milk and rearing goods. It is said to help in cases of anaemia and is one of the many aids to growth.

CHOLINE

Part of the *B complex*, choline is concerned with the metabolism of fat; together with pantothenic acid, it is necessary for the formation of acetylcholine which is so necessary for correct functioning of muscles, nerves, etc. It is found in yeast and milk.

It can be seen from this brief outline of nutrients how important the B group of vitamins is to the well-being of cockatiels, and all birds.

VITAMIN C (ASCORBIC ACID)

Cockatiels, like other seed-eating birds, can manufacture vitamin C within their bodies. However, it is included in some rearing foods and multi-vitamin tonic preparations. Vitamin C is contained in pollen and 'chinese leaf'; bean sprouts are also a rich source.

VITAMIN D2 and D3 (CALCIFEROL AND CHOLECALCIFEROL)

Two very important vitamins needed for the formation of bone and to enable the bird to transform the calcium and phosphorus taken into its body into substances it can absorb.

Peter C. Cragg D.V.M. Texas, writing in the *National Cockatiel Society's Journal* No. 3, June 1986, states 'Vitamin D2 is inactive in birds and can only be used when converted to Vitamin D3 by the action of sunlight on the bird's skin.' Vitamin D2 is easy and cheap to acquire from a veterinarian.

Collo-Cal D® oral is made by C. VET Ltd, Bury St Edmunds, UK, and is a great help to hand-reared birds, provided that they can be put in warm sunshine for a few minutes each day, or in the light provided by a form of electric light which emits ultraviolet rays.

Lack of the essential vitamin D3 will result in poor bone formation, poor health, poor hatching results, thin shelled eggs, and egg binding. Natural D3 is made by the action of sunlight on the bird's skin. Birds kept indoors, even with the benefit of light such as Tru-Lite should be given D3 in the form of a multi-vitamin preparation. The main source of D3 is cod liver oil, but I do not recommend using this substance: it is difficult to get the birds to eat seed impregnated with this substance as it goes rancid very quickly and then the birds will not eat the seed, or if they do, it will do them no good. D3 is found in eggs and is included in multi-vitamin tonics and in rearing foods. All breeding birds should be given D3 in some form before the breeding season to ensure that the hens are able to correct their calcium intake properly.

VITAMIN E (TOCOPHEROL)

This is sometimes referred to as the 'fertility vitamin'. It is included in rearing foods, multi-vitamin tonics and is present in green foods, grass seeds, and pollen.

VITAMIN K

This is needed to clot the blood, and is particularly necessary during the first two to three days of hand-rearing chicks from incubator-hatched eggs. A shortage of this vitamin could possibly occur if birds are subjected to prolonged courses of antibiotics, causing changes in the bacteria in the intestines which are normally able to 'manufacture' some vitamin K. One source of vitamin K is yoghourt; this is why very tiny quantities of yoghourt are recommended for very young baby cockatiels, and once per day also *before* giving antibiotics. Vitamin K is also found in most green leaves and in grass. It is included in rearing foods and vitamin tonics and is present in pollen.

CALCIUM

It would be impossible to overstate the importance of calcium or the necessity of maintaining as nearly as possible a correct calcium/phosphorus balance. As previously mentioned, it must be remembered that calcium and vitamin D3 are closely related. Without the action of vitamin D3 in some form or other in the body, the bird *cannot* convert its calcium intake into a substance which it can use for maintaining correct functions of the nerves, heart, blood vessels and egg laying. Lack of sufficient calcium, and vitamin D3 to convert it for the body's use is a major reason for egg binding. Calcium is a major constituent of bone, as well as muscles and nerves. Seeds tend to be low in calcium, but some green leaves such as spinach and dandelion contain a lot of this substance as do chicory and lettuce, although to a lesser degree. Sunflower seeds contain some calcium, but the best sources are cuttlefish bone, oystershell grit, and limestone grit. Calcium is also contained in milk, bread, oats and eggs, as well as in tonics for birds.

PHOSPHORUS

Phosphorus is closely linked with calcium and D3, and all three interrelate. This element is important in the metabolism of fats and carbohydrates, and is an important constituent of all living cells, especially muscle and in the formation of eggshell. Phosphorus is so widely distributed amongst foods it would only be possible to mention a few. Sunflower seeds contain this substance, as do cabbage, sprouts, spinach, lettuce and carrot, dandelion and chicory, milk, eggs, bread, oats and tonics.

Calcium/Phosphorus Ratio

The correct ratio of these two important minerals is: two parts calcium to one part phosphorus.

Necessary to the well-being of cockatiels and other seed-eating birds are a number of minerals in minute quantities, usually referred to as 'trace elements'. The fact that such small quantities are needed does not mean that they are not important. Many are vital to health. Some of the commonest are the following, although it should be noted that this is not the full list of trace elements used by birds.

IRON
An essential constituent of the blood. Increased quantities are needed for egg laying. Iron can be stored in the liver. It is present in 'mineralised' grits, rearing foods and sunflower seeds. Spinach, chicory, cabbage, dandelion and carrot all contain iron, which is also found in bread, oats, eggs, milk and tonics, and in pollen.

COPPER
Necessary during egg production, this is used by the bird's body in conjunction with proteins. It is included in rearing foods and mineralised grits, and is found in sunflower seeds and tonics and also pollen. Stewart Evans and Mike Fidler in their book *The Gouldian Finch* (published 1986 by Blandford Press, Artillery House, Artillery Row, London SW1P 1RT, England) state (p.64) that copper is required for the manufacture of the black pigment eumelanin.

MAGNESIUM
This is not found in the body to the same extent as calcium and phosphorus, but is an essential part of the bones of birds. It is needed by the bird to metabolise carbohydrates, and for eggshell formation. Magnesium is found in rearing foods, tonics, cabbage, spinach, lettuce and pollen.

POTASSIUM
Found in bone and other parts of the body and has a relaxing effect. It plays a part in the well-being of the heart, and in the healthy functioning of the red blood cells. It is contained in tonics and is found in sunflower seeds. Dandelion, chicory, pollen and lettuce all contain potassium.

IODINE
Used together with the amino acid tyrosine, by the thyroid gland in its manufacture of the hormone thyroxine. Together with manganese it is needed for egg production and it is included in tonics and rearing foods.

SODIUM WITH CHLORINE
Needed in tiny quantities to assist the body's digestive processes and the assimilation of iron. It is included in some tonics, in mineralised grit, and in some rearing foods.

SULPHUR

Contained in some of the amino acids, particularly methionine and cystine (see p.71) which are necessary constituents of eggs, and keratin, which is the essential ingredient of nails, beak (horny tissue), and is also necessary for feathers. It can thus be seen how necessary a good supply of methionine and cystine is for the perfect formation of the beak.

MANGANESE

With iodine, this is needed for egg production, as stated above. It is also needed to prevent dead in shell, and abnormalities of the bones. It is included in tonics and in rearing foods, and is contained in sunflower seeds.

ZINC

Necessary in tiny quantities for growth, and when large amounts of calcium are being used by the bird; it is included in rearing foods.

Some other minerals found, for example, in sunflower seeds are the following: sulphur is a constituent of some amino acids, fluorine in large quantities can be toxic to birds, selenium is said to prevent encephalomalacia (softening of the brain) and muscular dystrophy in poultry, molybdenum is necessary for normal growth, cobalt is not necessary for birds, providing that sufficient vitamin B12 is present in the diet, and chloride is best described as a part of chlorine.

The list of amino acids, vitamins and essential minerals given does not cover all the substances used by cockatiels when they consume their normal diet of seeds, green and root foods, plus all the 'extras' in the form of grit, tonics, cuttlefish bone, etc. However, it does perhaps give an insight into why, if some of these constituents of food are lacking, things can go so wrong. Seed merchants usually print the 'break-down' of their rearing foods on the packets; these should be studied to see what they contain. The same applies to vitamin supplements, and other tonics for birds.

Unfortunately it has not proved possible to obtain information regarding the exact mineral (ash) content of any of the basic seed foods needed for cockatiels, with the exception of sunflower, which was the subject of trials at the Department of Avian Sciences, University of California, Davis, about which G. R. Grau wrote in an article of 27 April 1985 in *Cage and Aviary Birds*. A brief summary of the content of sunflower kernels given by him is as follows. Approximately 49 per cent lipid (fat), 24 per cent protein, 21 per cent carbohydrate and 4 per cent ash (minerals) with small amounts of vitamins and other substances.

SUNFLOWER SEED

This appears to contain an appreciable amount of vitamin A. No vitamin D3, E, K or B12 is present, but thiamine (B1), riboflavin (B2), niacin and pyridoxine (B6) are all contained in sunflower seeds in small amounts, as is pantothenic acid. Minerals are represented by: iron, the largest amount, some manganese, potassium and phosphorus, with traces of copper and calcium. Other minerals are absent, or present in tiny amounts. Proteins are very well represented with 12 amino acids, including lysine, methionine and cystine and tyrosine.

CANARY SEED

Contains approximately 50 per cent carbohydrate, 14 per cent protein and approximately 15 per cent fat. It lacks the amino acid cystine altogether.

VARIOUS MILLETS

These contain approximately 60 per cent carbohydrate, 12 per cent protein, 4 per cent fat and 4 per cent minerals. They contain good quantities of all the essential amino acids including lysine, methionine and cystine, and tyrosine. Millets form an essential part of a cockatiel's diet.

RAPE SEED

Not usually thought of as a food for cockatiels and contains only 18 per cent carbohydrates but 20 per cent protein, 50 per cent fats-oils and 4 per cent minerals; the above figures are approximate.

NIGER SEED

Extremely useful to give to hens just before they are about to lay and until after the third egg is laid; it is an oily seed containing linoleic acid. It contains approximately 20 per cent protein, 40 per cent fats-oils and 13 per cent carbohydrates, minerals are very approximately 4 per cent. Because of its oily content it is very important that niger seed should be unbroken, fresh, and shiny black. When broken, it goes rancid, and is useless. It has good supplies of all the essential amino acids, including lysine, methionine and cystine and tyrosine.

HEMP SEED

Fortunately available to breeders of cockatiels in the UK but is not available in some parts of the world. It is a most useful 'cold weather' seed, provided that it is used very sparingly. If the temperature drops to 22°F (minus 4°C) or below, then I throw hemp seed on the ground at the rate of half a teaspoonful per bird, once daily, until the temperature rises to above freezing. The birds like it very much, and it cheers them up in cold, miserable weather. Too much of it would be liable to cause fatty livers and might also over-stimulate the hens, causing them to produce eggs far too early. It is low in carbohydrates, at approximately 18 per cent, not as high in fats-oils as niger, having very approximately 30 per cent, and approximately the same protein content at 19 per cent. Mineral content is nearly 5 per cent. It has good supplies of amino acids, including lysine, methionine and cystine, and tyrosine.

OATS
In the form of groats, which are oats which have had the husk removed, these are an excellent food for cockatiels, in small quantities. The carbohydrate content is approximately 60 per cent, protein 10 per cent, fats 5 per cent, minerals 3 per cent. Groats contain vitamin E (tocopherol) and also potassium and phosphorus. All the essential amino acids are present, including lysine, methionine and cystine, and tyrosine.

It is interesting to note part of the analysis of Prewett's 'Oat Bran and Oat Germ', which has been recommended for hand-rearing in Chapter 7. It is as follows: protein, approximately 16 per cent, carbohydrate, 60 per cent, fat, 9 per cent. Also contained in the above product is manganese, zinc, vitamins B1 (thiamine), B2 (riboflavin), and B6 (pyridoxine), and vitamin E (tocopherol).

LINSEED
Not a seed usually thought of for cockatiels, but if given in very small quantities it will be eaten, at least occasionally. It is used by canary breeders to give the feathers of their birds a shining attractive lustre. The approximate carbohydrate value is 22 per cent, fats-oils 34 per cent, protein 21 per cent, minerals 5 per cent. It appears to be quite well supplied with amino acids, including the essential ones mentioned above. Like niger it *must* be fresh and unbroken, as it can go rancid and in this condition be most injurious to the birds.

SAFFLOWER SEED
This has a very strong, rather bitter taste. It takes months to get cockatiels to eat this seed; and there seems little point in giving it when its values are so similar to sunflower, which the birds enjoy. Carbohydrates are approximately 16 per cent, minerals 3 per cent, fats 28 per cent, and protein 14 per cent. It contains all the essential amino acids, including lycine, methionine and cystine, and tyrosine.

The above list of seeds includes those likely to be used by breeders of cockatiels in the UK. Feeding very much depends on where the reader lives. Sydney, Australia, has a very different climate from London, England. The people of California or Florida will need to give their birds a different diet in the winter from those living in the

Northern states of the USA, and so on, all over the world. Diets must be adapted to local conditions, and local supplies. Green foods, too, vary enormously from country to country. Breeders of cockatiels, my husband and myself included, are always trying new combinations of foods, and in the case of young birds, sometimes new rearing methods. If we were asked to supply details of a good standard seed mix for cockatiels, we would have to ask 'In what country? What supplies are available?' Our own way of feeding is very different from that which has proved successful for many breeders. Therefore it must be pointed out that if the reader feels that the foods he or she is supplying are totally satisfactory, they should not be changed.

The cockatiels bred and kept in our aviaries are fed a diet which quite literally varies week by week, according to the time of year, the weather, and whether the birds are 'nesting', are just coming into breeding condition, or are actually rearing young.

Only one item of food is never varied: sunflower seed, striped and white mixed with a little small black sunflower, is given all year round. It is always fed separately from other seeds because of the large amount of dusty matter coming from the husks, is always given in unlimited quantities, and is renewed twice per day, winter and summer alike.

Canary seed is perhaps best thought of as a 'bread and butter' food, but remember that it lacks that important amino acid cystine. It is, however, a good source of carbohydrate, and when used with a selection of millet, makes, with sunflower, an excellent base seed diet for cockatiels. Opinions vary as to the ideal ratio of canary to millets; probably a good mix for most seasons and most climates would be 45 per cent canary seed to 55 per cent mixed millets. Groats are a most useful seed, and well liked by the birds, in small quantities. Many newcomers to cockatiels are inclined to think that cockatiels will rear their young on soaked groats. It is unlikely that this will lead to success. They do not like the seed enough to take it in sufficient quantities for rearing young. However, this should not deter the reader from including it as an extra item of diet. Black rape seed is useful, in very small quantities, and hemp seed is particularly useful as a warming 'treat' in cold weather. As a general rule hemp seed is never included in seeds given to our birds; being only used for special purposes for short periods of time. Linseed, like rape seed, is used in the seed mixture in really tiny quantities in the autumn and winter months only.

That excellent seed, niger, is also only used before egg-laying takes place and until the third or perhaps fourth egg is laid. It is far too 'forcing' a seed to be used continually. It must also be borne in mind that some rearing foods contain very small quantities of small hemp seed, and sometimes niger as well. We no longer give safflower seed;

the birds take a long time to acquire the taste for this bitter seed, and it would appear that sunflower can give the birds all the substances that are contained in safflower and more.

Seeds are the main diet of cockatiels, but it should not be forgotten that they need many other foods to complete their diet. Cuttlefish bone is vital, and should be supplied all year round, fresh and white. Scraped thinly when the hens are laying and the birds are feeding young, it is greatly appreciated by busy parents. Oyster shell grit must be supplied all year round, and fresh at least once per week, more often in the breeding season. Mineralised grits, which contain vital added minerals, need to be supplied in quantity and likewise renewed at least once per week, more often during breeding. It is noticeable that birds always want more mineralised grits in very cold weather.

Green foods are a difficult subject at the present. In the UK and in the USA, roadside verges are sprayed with poisonous chemicals. Farmers spray their crops with every kind of substance, many of which are lethal to birds. Market gardeners and even private gardeners, especially rose and fruit enthusiasts, are always spraying their plants. Since foregoing the pleasure of seeing the birds enjoy wild seeds and greens, our birds have been in such splendid health that it seems rather absurd to take the risk of giving them a 'treat' which may turn out to be a disease-carrying disaster (from wild birds), or a poisoned feed.

Our cockatiels are given daily wedges of carrot and celery, 'speared' on to headless nails, driven half way into wood uprights, near a convenient perch. Also supplied daily are some kind of cabbage or 'spring greens' (a form of cabbage) and lettuce. These greens are wired to the perches with very thin wire and when the weather is extremely hot and the birds are feeding young, it is renewed in the late afternoon. Chicory is a good food too, but our birds do not seem to care for it much. Cockatiels will eat turnip and swede, but not with any great enthusiasm. During the winter, to keep their minds off the cold, it is a good idea to give the birds a small, well-washed branch of either willow, hazelnut, or apple, taking care not to remove the buds on the branch but removing all the leaves, which is a great treat to cockatiels. Spray millet is good for this purpose too, provided that it is very clean.

For those who care to risk giving their birds wild foods, who have them growing in their gardens, or who know of a relatively safe source, some suggestions of excellent wild food is given below, which will no doubt be greatly enjoyed by cockatiels. Dandelion seeding heads are particularly good for cockatiels, especially when they are feeding young. Do *not* give them the stalks or any but the very smallest and youngest leaves. I have known grass parakeets die after eating dandelion stalks. Seeding grasses are much appreciated, but do not give the birds any kind with long spiky outer covering; these can stick in the birds' throats, and kill them. Knapweed *(Centaurea)* seeding heads, stalks, and leaves will all be devoured by cockatiels; so too will the seeding heads of sow thistle *(Sonchus oleraceus)*. The seeding heads of the various hawkweeds *(Hieracium)* are enjoyed, but not to the same extent as the other plants mentioned above.

Chickweed *(Stellaria media)* so beloved by so many smaller birds is a good wild food, but must be given very fresh. It may harbour the eggs of the threadworm *Capillaria;* since Rosemary Low warned of this danger, I have stopped giving it to our cockatiels. Persicaria and its relative knotgrass, both members of the *Polygonum* family, are eaten by some cockatiels, not by others. Dock seeds of the commonest kind of dock *(Rumex obtusifolius)* are appreciated by cockatiels, but beware of the wild sorrels, also members of the *Rumex* family, as they contain too much oxalic acid for good health. Plantain seeding heads are sometimes liked, the Latin name is *Plantago major.*

Two flowers grown in gardens all over the UK are greatly enjoyed by cockatiels when seeding. One is that old favourite of gardeners, the forget-me-not *(Myosotis)*, the other is the common marigold *(Calendula officinalis)*. Seeding heads of spinach are extremely good for cockatiels, and very much appreciated, as are any seeding greens, such as lettuce and the various cabbages. Cress is eaten, but apparently not with much enthusiasm, and similarly sprouted mung beans; the birds will eat them, but tire of these two foods very quickly. Some people say that cockatiels like apple, but I have never yet found one who will eat this or any other fruit.

Perhaps one of the foods most near to part of their natural diet in the wild, and one which cockatiels invariably like is pollen, provided that it is in its natural state, contained in fresh flowers; for example apple, willow, or even 'gum' tree *(Eucalyptus)* all produce beautiful flowers, full of pollen, which is of immense value to the birds. James D. Ford from Salt Lake City, Utah, USA, writing in the *American Federation of Aviculture's Journal,* of April-May 1982, states that pollen contains 25 per cent protein, and all 22 amino acids. He gives a long list of every sort of vitamin, an impressive list of minerals, and an equally long list of other important substances. Pollen can be bought in the UK at health food shops, but it is very expensive. By far the best way to give it to the birds is on a branch. Cockatiels will devour every bit of pussy willow flower and forget-me-not flower.

A word of warning here: very many common garden flowers and shrubs are poisonous; do not experiment, without first checking to make sure that the flower intended for the cockatiels contains no poison. Certain kinds of honeysuckle are poisonous, the black honeysuckle *(Lonicera niga)* and the fly honeysuckle *(Lonicera xylosteum)* are both considered dangerous for children. But the common wild honeysuckle, which grows in hedgerows in the southern parts of the UK is quite harmless (its Latin name is *Lonicera periclymenum).* The beautifully-scented flowers are greatly enjoyed by many cockatiels, who also enjoy the young shoots very much.

Cockatiels will enjoy eating various berries, especially mountain ash *(Sorbus aucuparia),* also those of the hawthorn *(Crataegus monogyna);* but in the latter case be sure to remove all those terrible 'spikes' from the branches. The berries of the wild elder *(Sambucus nigra)* are a great treat to cockatiels, but remember the juice of the berries can stain their plumage. Jim Hayward, writing in his journal, *Parrot Breeder,* No.6, 1985 warns his readers that the dwarf elder *(Sambucus ebulus)* is regarded as poisonous; he also very rightly warns of the dangers of that thoroughly poisonous tree the laburnum, 'golden chain' or golden rain as it is sometimes known. Its Latin name is *Laburnum anagyroides.* The poisonous seeds are a particular danger to cockatiels. The yew *(Taxus baccata)* is extremely poisonous, and the bark of the silver birch *(Betula pendula)* is said to be bad for parrot-type birds, as is the bark of oak *(Quercus).* Ivy *(Hedera)* is another plant to avoid, as it is considered poisonous.

The list of garden plants, shrubs, and trees which are either poisonous or very injurious to cockatiels and other parrot-type birds is endless. The best plan is to keep all shrubs, trees, and climbers well away from aviaries, and make inquiries about any particular plant if in doubt. I only know of one parrot-type bird that is, so far, a reliable 'poison taster', that is the turquoisine grass parrakeet *(Neophema pulchella);* if these little birds refuse to eat some wild or garden plant, then that plant is best left well alone.

Cockatiels will benefit very greatly from a vitamin and mineral tonic, given during the winter and spring months. There are many made especially for birds, some in powder form, but water soluble, others in liquid form for adding to the drinking water, yet others made to sprinkle over the food. One of the water soluble ones I have found excellent is Solvit®, a multi-vitamin preparation made by Micro-Biologicals Ltd., Fordingbridge, Hampshire, England. It contains a lot of vitamin D3, and is the best way I know to ensure that the hens are 'stocked up' with that vital substance. It only has to be given four times each winter at intervals at least a week apart, at the rate of one large teaspoonful to two gallons (10 litres) of water. Leave for 24 hours, then renew, then give another dose a week or two weeks later. This preparation must be obtained from a veterinarian. I am indebted to the well known veterinarian and aviculturalist Mr George Smith MRCVS for this information.

Another vitamin and mineral additive, which can be bought at pet shops in the UK is SA37. It is manufactured primarily for cats and dogs, but is excellent for birds and can be given to them too.

A word of advice to newcomers to cockatiel breeding, on the subject of buying and storing seeds. Firstly, do buy the best quality available; it always pays. Seeds, all seeds, should be shiny and clean, and should sprout if soaked in water and kept warm for several days. Secondly, do store the seed in the coolest, driest place available in containers with good firm lids, which really do fit. Those who buy in large quantities will find that new clean dustbins (garbage cans) with good fitting lids are excellent containers for seeds.

9 Hygiene

Hygiene is an aspect of cockatiel management which is unfortunately sadly neglected by some newcomers, and, even worse, by some well-established breeders. Not until disaster hits them in the form of some infectious disease will some people realise the importance of keeping everything clean.

The best way to practise hygiene with cockatiels is by daily sweeping and cleaning of the aviaries. Birds kept this way will be living in far more hygienic conditions than those whose owners do a huge spring or autumn 'clean out' with some strong disinfectant solutions. Obviously the ideal would be to practise both methods of maintenance. Birds kept in houses and flights which are kept constantly swept and cleaned, or perhaps brushed and cleaned with water, are much less likely to become feather pluckers than those which are only occasionally cleaned. Look at the way aviaries are kept in any really well known and well run zoo or bird garden; they are immaculately clean.

NEST BOXES
As soon as the nest boxes are removed at the end of the breeding season is a good time to give a thorough cleaning to both houses and flights. A brush down with a small stiff brush will remove any surface dirt and dust plus cobwebs. The daily removal of droppings is recommended, but if this is done less often it will be necessary to scrape the areas where these collect and remove them.

The whole of the interior of the houses, and all woodwork, feeding shelves and perches in the flights, as well, should be sprayed with a pressure sprayer. These can be bought at many garden centres. There are many excellent insecticides especially made for use in bird and animal houses. Especially dirty wooden surfaces may need the attention of a strong scrubbing brush. After an insecticide has been used it is as well to wipe the perches and feeding shelves dry with a cloth.

If an infectious disease has afflicted the birds it may be necessary to remove them all and go over all woodwork, perches etc. with a blowlamp. A veterinarian should be able to advise in such a case on the best course of action.

Nest boxes should always be taken down at the end of the season. The very valuable 'fertiliser' material contained in them can be put round rose trees or on a vegetable garden with great advantage to the plants. Having thoroughly cleaned out the boxes, they should then be soaked for 48 hours in a garbage bin filled with water, to which has been added a liberal amount of very strong disinfectant. I use Jeyes Parozone®. The boxes must be well washed out with water once they are removed so that no Parozone® remains. They can then be dried and stored away in a warm dry place until they are needed again.

Cockatiels are not particularly subject to feather mites, but if these trying little objects attack a bird, a bath in a Vanodine V18 solution may help to cure the problem. It is advisable to wear gloves for this task. Fill a bowl or sink with enough luke-warm water for the bird to stand with its shoulders just covered. Colour the water deep yellow with Vanodine®, put the bird in the bath and make it really soaking wet with repeated applications of the water and Vanodine. Protect the eyes, nostrils and beak with one hand. See to it that the head is made thoroughly wet and pay particular attention to any bare patches on the bird. Incidentally bare patches on the backs of lutino's heads are a genetic fault, *not* the result of feather mites or even feather plucking. After the bath, wrap the bird in a warm towel with its head protruding for air, then put it in a warm clean cage in a warm room to dry. In cold weather do not return it to its aviary until it is completely dry right down to the skin.

ENDING A BIRD'S LIFE PAINLESSLY

Everyone who keeps birds knows that there are occasions when it is kinder to say goodbye to a particular bird rather than to allow it to suffer to the bitter end. Sometimes, too, one has to consider the risks of infection to the rest of the flock. Or it may be that a much cherished pet is desperately ill or has suffered some terrible accident from which there appears to be no hope of recovery. In either case if possible a veterinarian should be consulted. These dedicated men and women will nearly always try to save a bird's life, but when the situation is hopeless they should be asked to put the bird painlessly out of its suffering. Where a veterinarian suspects an infectious disease it is better to sacrifice one bird than put all the other birds at risk.

Breeders of cockatiels who have many birds cannot, in the nature of things, rush off to the veterinarian every time something happens to make it advisable to humanely destroy a bird. No one likes to undertake this task, but it is as well to know how to undertake it without the bird suffering further.

Birds, like children and dogs, are psychic and will quickly 'pick up' any conversations about their future, or lack of it, with another person. Do *not* discuss the bird's future in front of it, especially if it is a pet bird. Make ready the arrangements for 'putting it to sleep' out of the bird's sight. A critically ill or wounded bird will be very docile, but nevertheless if it is an adult bird it would be wise to wear a light rubber glove on the hand which is going to hold the bird.

A bucket of water will be needed, and a jar or cup containing about 30 millilitres of pure Scotch Whisky. Fill a ten millilitre syringe, preferably one with a tube attached, with whisky, and either have another one handy also filled up, or be prepared to refill the first one. Insert the tube into the bird's throat, or if this is not available, put the nozzle of the syringe in the side of the bird's mouth and gently press the plunger 'home'. If it is a young bird 10 millilitres of whisky will probably be sufficient to make it unconscious. An adult bird, especially a large one, may easily require 20 or even 30 millilitres to reach this state. A bird which is rendered unconscious does not close its eyes. Do not imagine the bird knows at this stage what is going on; it does not. When the head rolls back put the bird under the water and hold it there for at least one minute, or better, for two minutes. Any movements at this stage will not be causing the bird any suffering. Its sufferings were over with the first few millilitres of pure whisky. A bird 'put to sleep' in this way should be wrapped up in several layers of newspaper then put into at least two plastic bags securely tied, if it is to be put in a garbage container. If it is a pet bird and a 'burial' is desired, see that it is at least 18 in (0.5 m) under ground. This will avoid foxes and other predators disturbing the little grave.

WORMING

It would be impossible to overestimate the importance of worming cockatiels. Probably more birds die as a result of being infested with worms of various kinds than for any other reason. It is not difficult to worm a cockatiel, which is after all, quite small and, provided that one wears a good lined glove on the hand which will hold the bird and lets it bite the glove to its heart's content, there should be no problems. There are people who say that they simply *cannot* bring themselves to worm a bird, and if they cannot get a competent and experienced person to help them, then rather than leave the birds entirely without worm medicine it would be best to get one of those advertised which can be added to the water and follow the directions given.

The three commonest kinds of worms which can be picked up by parrot-like birds in various stages of their development are large roundworms *(Ascaridia)*, threadworms or hairworms *(Capillaria)* and, according to Arnell and Keymer in their book *Bird Diseases*, one species of tapeworm *(Raillietina)*.

The first two mentioned are by far the most important to control; they are likely to do immense damage to the bird's health. Roundworms are whitish in colour, and usually up to 1 in (2.5cm) in length, although they can attain nearly four times that size.

The eggs of the worm are passed in the droppings of infected birds, and can then be picked up by the other inmates of an aviary. They will then lodge in the intestines of their new victim and develop into adult worms and multiply, making the bird lose condition and sometimes causing a complete blockage of the intestines. Direct sunlight kills the worms eggs; it is the damp shady areas of an aviary which will keep the eggs of these parasites alive.

Threadworms or hairworms vary in size from approximately $\frac{1}{2}$ in (1.3 cm) to 3 in (8 cm) in length and are like little bits of hair in appearance. They live in various parts of the body, including the crop and intestines. Like roundworms, the eggs are passed in the droppings of infected birds. A bird with a few of these worms is likely to have a poor appetite and be generally out of condition; one heavily infected has less chance of survival.

One sign of the presence in large numbers of these worms is yellow or blood-stained droppings but it must be remembered that this could be a symptom of various diseases, and not necessarily connected with worms.

The third parasite which may affect cockatiels is one kind of tapeworm. This varies in length from about $\frac{1}{4}$ in (0.63 cm) to about $13\frac{3}{4}$ in (35 cm). These ghastly objects are likely to bury themselves in the intestines and will seek nourishment from the bird. They consist of a long chain of segments, of which various sections produce eggs, in thousands.

As with the others worms, the eggs are expelled in the droppings and can be picked up by aviary inhabitants such as ants, earthworms, and slugs and snails which will be found in grass-covered flights. Many cockatiels, especially young ones, will pick at any of the above creatures, thus infecting themselves with eggs which eventually become tapeworms again.

Excessive thirst, loss of appetite and hence weight can be signs of the presence of these pests, but these symptoms may also herald the presence of various diseases.

Of the various types of worms commonly attacking cockatiels the tapeworm would probably be the most difficult to eradicate if the eggs should ever find their way into a bird's body. Fortunately, improved methods of worming, and more important, improved worm medicines, offer a much better chance of destroying all the above mentioned parasites than was the case a few years ago.

There are many good worm medicines suitable for birds available now; some, like the well tried Nemicide® containing Levamisole®, are good for controlling roundworms.

For some years now I have used Panacur®, made by Hoechst at Milton Keynes. It contains Fenbendazole®, and is made in two strengths. I use the weaker one, the 2.5 solution without trace additives; unopened it has a life of about four years, but once opend it should be used within a year (with the cap well screwed on) and kept in a cool dark place, but not in a refrigerator. It has a considerable sediment, so must be well shaken before use.

To make an easy-to-give dose I put one part of Panacur (the 2.5 solution) to ten parts of water; this then consititutes the ready-to-use worm medicine. The required dose for an adult cockatiel is one millilitre of this mixture, and half a millilitre for a young bird between two to four months old.

Putting worm medicine of any kind in the birds' water is not an effective way to worm them; cockatiels, like any number of Australian parrot-like birds, can go for several days without water in a cool climate, and even if they all drink the water which contains the medicine, how does one know how much each bird has taken? The same is true of putting it in food. If they do not like the taste of the food they will go without, and thus weaken themselves just when all their strength is needed for good breeding.

Cockatiels quickly get used to the twice-yearly worming sessions; indeed, if one should get overlooked out of a shelter full of cockatiels, that bird will almost certainly flap around one's head until it has had the same treatment as the others!

I use a 5 or 10 millilitre syringe with the hypodermic needle removed. Those trying their hand worming for the first time would be wise to practise without a tube attached to the syringe. Hold the bird in a gloved hand with the first finger on top of its head and the rest of the hand around its shoulders and front.

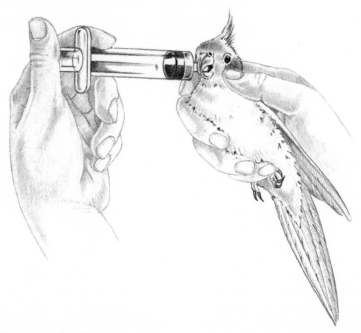

Worming a cockatiel.

Allow the bird to rest its feet firmly on your chest and also allow it to bite the glove. This opens its mouth, and the nozzle of the syringe can then be gently inserted into the side of the mouth, and the plunger pushed slowly 'home'.

Sometimes the liquid may squirt too fast down the bird's throat, which causes it to let some of the medicine out through the nostrils, and out into its eyes. Do not panic! It will be perfectly all right, and the eyes will not be damaged. One or two drops more can be given to correct the dose.

Those who have some experience of worming cockatiels with a syringe may prefer to use a tube to insert a short way down the throat. The tube I use is a very small electrical cable, called a single core multi-strand; and the reference number is 249 Ix. There are probably others equally good. Cut off about 2 in (5 cm) and extract all the wires; then make the cable just hot enough to soften, by soaking in hot water, and pull one end over the nozzle of the syringe enough to make it secure.

Cut the cable back to about $1\frac{1}{2}$ in (4 cm) and bend it slightly so that it goes down the throat easily; finally, file the edges of the cable so that it is smooth in the bird's throat.

When using a tube it is best to guide it straight over the tongue from the front of the beak, then very gently down the throat about 1 in (2.5 cm). I believe that more than this is unnecessary.

When worming with a tube, you will find that the birds 'close' their throats at first, but with patience and talking or whistling to them, they soon relax and allow the smooth passage of the tube without damage to the throat. Once the tube is down, the plunger should be pressed home immediately, and the sooner the tube is removed the better.

It does not seem to matter at all what time of day the worming is done, although I prefer to do it in the early morning on fairly empty crops. Cockatiels receiving Panacur® for the first time may not be quite at their best for two or three days, but thereafter should be perfectly well.

The worms and eggs, if there are any, are expelled dead, slowly over a period of many days. This means that there is no likelihood of a bird dying as a result of the worm medicine causing many worms to be expelled all at once, and possibly producing a total blockage in the intestines.

DEALING WITH MICE
Mouse-traps are unfortunately an essential item of equipment for the breeder of cockatiels. The floor can be of cement or stone slabs, the aviary flights can be double wired with the smallest mesh wire or weldmesh, but still the occasional minute baby mouse will somehow squeeze through somewhere, and eat for a day or perhaps more.

Then it is too big to get out again. The excreta of mice does not kill birds, but the urine, contaminating seeds or bits of grit and green food, etc., can and does kill. The best way to deal with this problem is to buy one of the box-type mousetraps, which once set will trap up to a dozen or more mice at a time. Unless the owner of the birds lives in a large city the type of little animals most likely to penetrate aviaries are field mice. These are extremely attractive little creatures with large eyes and ears. A journey into a country area is well worth while to release these little animals where they can do no harm. Box-type mousetraps which kill victims by slow drowning should be avoided; they are extremely cruel.

INSECTS

Compost heaps should be sited as far away from the aviaries as possible or avoided altogether. The reason is that during the warm summer months various types of midges and mosquitoes breed in such an environment and many of them are carriers of disease. They may bite a diseased cat, fox, squirrel or mouse and then go and feed on the blood of the cockatiels, both old and young. This can lead to all kinds of trouble, from anaemia to certain diseases which can be transmitted by insects.

On the subject of gnats, mosquitoes, etc., it is worth noting that non-poisonous spiders should be encouraged in houses and flights. They dispose of a lot of tiresome insects.

One of the worst enemies of all bird keepers and breeders is the little grey insect known as red mite. It lives in crevices in woodwork and comes out at night to suck the blood of birds as they sleep on perches or in nest boxes. The least that can happen is severe anaemia, the worst is that the birds can contract a nasty disease called lankesterella previously called atoxoplasma. This scourge can be controlled by the frequent use of any of the many liquids and aerosol sprays especially made to deal with red mite.

There are many different mites which attack birds, either sucking their blood, or devouring parts of their feathers, often causing intense irritation, and causing affected birds to pull out their feathers. These can now be controlled by the use of any of the many insecticides especially manufactured for that purpose.

FLOOR HYGIENE

Where the general hygiene of the floor of houses and flights is concerned it should be borne in mind that nothing is as effective as *daily* scraping up of droppings and sweeping of the floors. Cockatiels do not have such a definite moult as do many birds. They tend to lose a few feathers at a time, all the year round, and then lose rather more towards the end of their breeding season. Much trouble caused by the nasty habit of feather plucking out of boredom or for fun, can be avoided if the birds are not tempted by finding feathers on the floor of the aviary which they then pick up and chew.

Droppings, provided they are from absolutely healthy birds, and provided they are dust dry are probably, like those of healthy domestic fowls, quite antiseptic. But in northern European climates how often are they completely dry? The answer is, only in a 'heat wave'. Hosing floors with water is quite a good measure, provided that the areas hosed are also swept thoroughly. If this is not done, the water mixing with dirt and droppings will do more harm than good, due to the damp conditions activating germs which would otherwise die, particularly in direct sunlight.

10 First Aid

Anyone who has been very ill in a hospital will know how much their successful recovery depended on good nursing by dedicated, understanding nurses. It is all very well for the doctor or specialist to come and make their respective pronouncements, but later, perhaps in the dead of night or the early hours of the morning when a crisis looms, where does the responsibility lie? With the nurse in charge.

Owners of sick or injured birds are in the position of the nurse. A veterinarian can diagnose, advise, prescribe, but he or she cannot be there when the bird's physical resources and will to live may be running at a very low ebb.

It is then that so much depends on the owner's or keeper's observation and ability to vary the treatment to suit a particular situation. It may be that a particular antibiotic has been prescribed which is not suiting the bird and another one could be substituted. It may be that a bird pines for its mate, and the sight of the mate, brought in to see the ill one for a few minutes gives it heart to fight for its life.

Sometimes it is just a word or a whistle of encouragement from the owner which makes all the difference to the bird's recovery. It is these things coupled with the skilled help of the veterinarian which may well mend a broken or diseased little body.

DEALING WITH A DEAD BIRD

Whether an afflicted bird has suffered an accident of some kind, or is in fact suffering from some as yet undiagnosed disease can be determined by a quick check of the bird when it is picked up or caught. If the bird is dead, check first if its neck has been broken by a severe fright of some kind.

In this case, when the bird is held in the hand the neck will 'roll' from side to side. If this does not appear to be the case and there is no visible damage, for the sake of the rest of the owner's flock, it may be thought worthwhile to have a post mortem.

If possible, birds should be taken to an establishment which can carry out this work as quickly as possible; within an hour is ideal. In some cases it may be impossible for the person doing the post mortem to determine what is wrong with the bird if it has first been taken to a veterinarian who does not undertake this work, and who, perhaps refrigerates the bird, then sends it through the post to be autopsied.

It should also be remembered that in order to arrive at a diagnosis it may be necessary to do quite a lot of work, involving perhaps several days' wait to see the result of cultures. This can in some cases be costly, but is well worthwhile if the owner's flock of birds is at risk.

NURSING, TONICS AND MEDICINES
When the owner is concerned with a live bird which appears to be ill, two things are vital: warmth and water. An ill bird, or a bird suffering from shock needs immediate warmth, 80-85°F (27-29°C), plus water. An ill bird is often very dehydrated.

Do *not* put tonics, medicines, etc., in the bird's drinking water, which will almost certainly stop it drinking. It is by drinking that the bird may save its life. Any medicines, etc., are best given straight into the mouth. Ill birds soon get used to being handled and are grateful for the help they are receiving, especially when it is given with an encouraging word. I have literally saved the lives of countless birds over the years by getting them to 'fight back' themselves.

ACCIDENTS
A bird who has met with an accident needs instant attention. An apparently broken wing or leg calls for immediate veterinary help. A broken wing is best secured with a strip of sheeting or other material wrapped securely round it and tied; or if this fails to hold the broken part, wrap the bird in a towel with its head and legs protruding, and prop it up in a moderately warm cage. Remember the bird will be hot with a towel covering.

In the case of a bird with a leg completely broken off, it will go into shock very quickly. Tape the wounded leg with dressing strip, enough to form a firm 'stump', and put the bird on a soft towel in a cage with a temperature of 85°F (30°C).

In either of the above cases, before putting the bird in its cage give it two beakfuls of glucose and lukewarm water. Half a teaspoon of glucose to a tablespoon of water, over the bird's tongue, given with a syringe or spoon will help to keep the bird alive through the initial shock. Two drops of brandy in the first half teaspoon of drink would also help. The glucose and water must be given every two hours, leaving the bird about five hours to sleep at night. In both cases warmth and soft flooring in the cage are essential.

POISONS
In the case of a poisoned bird a steady flow of liquid through it can quite possibly save its life. Larger parrots who have eaten poisoned seed have been known to save their lives by constantly drinking. When a bird which was perfectly well the day before is found huddled up on the floor of an aviary or cage, one could suspect some kind of poisoning.

The urine of mice kills birds very fast indeed, although the excreta

93

is not nearly so harmful. Seed or green food which has been contaminated with poisonous sprays is another obvious cause of the bird's illness to be considered

Until a veterinarian can be consulted, the best thing to do would be to put the bird in a warm cage, and keep the temperature up to around 85°F (30°C). Give it two or three mouthfuls of the glucose and water mixture ($\frac{1}{2}$ teaspoon of glucose in one tablespoon of lukewarm water) every two hours, leaving the bird with about five to six hours sleep during the night.

The reader may wonder 'why the glucose?' The answer is simple, it gives the bird immediate sugar, and sugar is strength.

ILLNESSES

A bird which has appeared off-colour for some time and sits huddled on its perch, or quite possibly eats as though its life depended on it (which it does), and which has a 'knife edge' breastbone could be suffering from worms, or from a disease, or from overtaxing its strength by over-breeding and a badly balanced diet. These are some of the possibilities which come to mind, but a veterinarian must be consulted.

Birds suffering from the disease variously known as pseudotuberculosis, yersinia pseudotuberculosis, or pasteurella pseudotuberculosis will very likely also have a 'knife edge' breastbone, but will not eat madly. Birds suffering from the above disease will suffer from acute depression, rendering them immobile for hours at a time. The outlook is not good, and the risk to the rest of the flock considerable. A veterinarian must be consulted at the earliest possible time.

PSITTACOSIS

Everybody wants to know if their ill bird is suffering from psittacosis; it is endemic, and regularly found in Europe, Great Britain included, and in most other parts of the world as well.

A bird huddled up with ruffled plumage and closed eyes which discharge watery matter is best got away from other birds, and children too, as rapidly as possible. It may not be psittacosis, probably not; but consult a veterinarian immediately, it is better to be safe than sorry.

It is not possible to diagnose psittacosis for certain except by a post mortem. Sad as it may be, if the bird in question is thought to be suffering from this disease, and there are children around; it would be better to say goodbye to the bird. Progress is being made all the time in the treatment of this illness.

If the owner is told by the veterinarian that the bird in question did in fact suffer from psittacosis, he or she, plus any family, should immediately consult their doctor, who will very likely take blood tests and prescribe a course of antibiotic treatment. Oxytetracycline might be used.

FEATHER PLUCKING

Feather plucking of young by their parents is an infuriating trait which may appear quite unexpectedly. No-one seems to know yet whether feather plucking is the result of stress, dietary deficiency, or some other cause. Certainly birds which are allowed to breed when very young, especially hens, seem more prone to this troublesome behaviour. Very often a young hen may have grossly overtaxed her strength; she needs the fat at the base of the quills of her nestlings, so she starts to take one or two; but the habit rapidly grows. Before long the cock joins in (feather plucking is very catching) and soon the owner will find a nestful of bare and sometimes bleeding chicks. The only thing to do is to spray the young twice a day with any good 'anti-peck' aerosol.

Birds who feather pluck at other times may be 'over-preening' their mates; in which case the above treatment applies to both birds. A powder containing the B complex of vitamins, sprinkled on the food for several months would do a lot to ease the problem. Birds who feather pluck are often stressed birds, and can be greatly helped by the various B vitamins.

Really bad feather pluckers are best disposed of as soon as possible, it is a bad habit, and will rapidly spread to other birds. Larger parrots have been successfully treated for this condition; I do not refer to it as a vice, because it could be the cause is something lacking in the diet of the birds, or their management.

The treatment of the large parrots consisted of giving a 'knife's tip full' of common salt in 500 millilitres of water daily. The birds concerned all drank the water, and one stopped feather plucking at once, the others did so in the course of a few months. I would not recommend this treatment for breeding birds who are feeding their young.

CROSSED TOES

Young birds who come out of the nest with crossed claws or toes can be helped by giving them small diameter ($\frac{1}{2}$ in – 1.27 cm) square perches instead of round ones. If they are not suffering from rickets and are quite healthy this will be found very helpful to them. Curling toes can be a sign of lack of vitamin B, and adding vitamin B to the food of some non-parrot-like species has been known to alleviate this condition.

EGG-BINDING

Cockatiels are hardy birds and if properly housed and fed are not particularly likely to suffer from egg-binding; but it is as well to be prepared, and to keep a careful watch on laying hens in cold weather. Usually if there is going to be a problem, it will not be with the first egg, but much more likely with the third, or even the fourth.

Some experiments conducted by myself and my husband seemed to suggest that cockatiels are not capable of sustaining sufficient heat to hatch their eggs at temperatures below 40°F (5°C). Added to the problem of dead in shell, due to the cold, the hens are much more likely to become egg-bound.

When a hen is found in this condition, she usually comes out of the nest and goes to the floor, exhausted. Action should be immediate, put her on a warm towel in a cage with a temperature of 85-90°F (30-34°C). Give her sips, two or three beakfuls at a time, of glucose and water, half a teaspoon of glucose to one tablespoon of luke warm water. Repeat every two hours.

The bird should be given a few hours to see if the warmth and glucose and water will strengthen her sufficiently to enable her to lay the egg herself.

If she has been kept in overnight and is still straining in the morning, it might be that either a soft shelled egg, or some obstruction is making it impossible for her to lay her egg, in this case she should be attended to by a veterinarian.

An apparently hopeless case of an exhausted hen with a weak heart beat, and almost unconscious, was rendered temporarily unaware of the stress and pain of the necessary probing by a skilled veterinarian by giving her two beakfuls of pure brandy. Just before the probing to find the cause of the obstruction she was given the brandy, and half way through her (and my) ordeal her heart stopped; it was immediately massaged, and started again; a minute or so later two more beakfuls of brandy were dripped into her.

With some help a huge soft-shelled egg ejected about eight hours later. The assistance consisted of inserting a fairly stiff tube attached to a syringe about ½in (1.27cm) into the vent, having first put a little olive oil or vaseline around the area, and injecting a saline douch. When about 10-20 millilitres of this douche had been administered, and come out again; the soft-shelled and by now broken egg shot out.

The saline douch was prepared by putting one teaspoon of salt to one teacup of lukewarm water. After the egg was expelled this brave little hen was given two beakfuls of pure brandy, and put in a temperature of 95°F (34°C). Four hours later this was dropped to 90°F (31°C) and the above-mentioned glucose and water was continued. Six hours later half a teaspoon of Prewett's® oatbran and oatgerm (from health food shops) was added to form a very thin 'soup'. Another six hours later half a teaspoon of Milupa® Autumn Fruit Harvest (baby food) was added to form a slightly thicker mix, and as before, fed every two hours, except for five hours' sleep during the night.

Colony aviary.

Two blocks of aviaries with flower beds.

Normal cock, property of Mr Terry Cole.

Normal hen, property of Mr Terry Cole.

Lutino cock, bred by the authors.

Lutino hen, bred by the authors.

Lutino Pearl hen; bred by the authors.

Lutino Pearl hen, property of Mr Leslie Gedge.

Pair of Cinnamons, property of Mr Bob Crossley.

Pair of Primrose Cinnamon Pieds, bred by the authors.

Cinnamon Lacewing hen, property of Mr Bob Crossley.

Cinnamon Pearl hen, bred by Miss **Barbara** Ball.

Primrose Cinnamon Pied hen, bred by the authors.

Primrose Cinnamon Pearl Pied cock, bred by the authors.

Primrose Cinnamon Pearl Pied hen, bred by the authors.

Primrose Cinnamon Lacewing Pied hen, bred by the authors.

Two young birds just out of their nests; Primrose Cinnamon Pearl Pied and Lutino Pearl. Bred by the authors.

Pearl hen, bred by the authors.

Heavily marked Primrose Pearl Pied hen, bred by the authors.

Pair of Primrose Pearl Pieds, bred by the authors.

Primrose Pearl Pied cock, bred by the authors.

A pair of Primrose Pearl Pieds and a heavily Pearled Pied hen, bred by the authors.

Primrose Pied cock, bred by the authors.

Primrose 'Heavy Pied' cock, bred by the authors.

Primrose Pied hen, bred by the authors.

Pair of White faced, property of Mr Bob
Crossley.

White faced cock, property of Mr Bob
Crossley.

Pied White faced cock and Pearl Pied White faced hen, property of Mr Bob Crossley.

Cinnamon White faced hen, property of Mr Terry Cole.

Albino, property of Mr Bob Crossley.

Dominant Silver cock, property of Mr Terry Cole.

A pet cockatiel, bred by the authors.

Pair of Dominant Silvers, property of Mr Terry Cole.

Hand-feeding of young.

A nest of Pearl young, bred by the authors.

Two days later the little hen was fed every four hours, but towards the end of the day she became very ill with some respiratory infection. She had running nostrils, a 'gurgling' throat, and closed eyes. The heat was kept at 90°F (34°C), a quarter of a millilitre of pure yoghourt was given each morning first thing, and two hours later one drop of Panmycine Aquadrops®, repeated in the evening, was dropped on the hen's tongue. The yoghourt and Panmycine were continued for five days, and this cured her; gradually normal food was offered, but she was also fed with a syringe for two more weeks with the Milupa®, glucose and oatbran mixture.

The ratio was two parts Milupa fruit harvest, one part oatbran and oatgerm, and one sixteenth part glucose mixed to a runny consistency. The above mentioned Milupa® food is excellent for birds, possibly because it contains a lot of vitamins, including D3, fruits which include blackberries, which birds like very much, and maize. The oatbran, apart from being an excellent food for cockatiels, added essential 'rough material' necessary to aid digestion.

The little hen refused to eat from a spoon, so the nozzle of an ordinary hypodermic syringe was bored with a tiny round file, so that it was enlarged just sufficiently to allow the rough oatbran to pass through.

At the end of ten days she suddenly started to eat, and on the twelfth day she spent the day in her aviary but was returned to the warmth of her cage each night for a further two days. During the whole of her illness her mate, a fine, large cock, was brought up to see her every day, but never left with her.

Subsequently this wonderful bird, after a long period of rest, reared two broods of five chicks each. She had no more problems with eggs, and three months after her ordeal was as sleek and beautiful as ever.

ANTIBIOTICS

For whatever reason antibiotics are given, and whichever kind is used; it should be noted that while these chemicals are used to kill harmful germs, they also kill necessary ones: particularly those called 'flora' in the gut, or intestines.

When antiobiotics are being given, in order to counteract this harmful action, give the bird to be medicated two beakfuls of pure yoghourt (about one quarter of a millilitre). Give this two hours *before* the first daily dose of antibiotic, and give it every day, once per day, that the bird takes whatever antibiotic has been prescribed. This will enable the bird to grow helpful bacteria in its intestines.

All the antibiotics are best given for five days, then a five day rest, then a further five days if really necessary. It is often quite unnecessary to give birds a longer course of medicine than the above-mentioned, and they will be all the better for being allowed to recover from an illness at their own pace, with warmth and good food.

DAMAGED CLAWS OR TOES
Sometimes a claw or a toe may be damaged and bleed profusely. This can be stopped by first washing it in very cool water, then applying Stiptick®; or dipping a tissue into some wet crystals of permanganate of potash, and dabbing the tissue on the bleeding part. These crystals can be obtained from a pharmacy or chemist.

CUTTING CLAWS
Aviary birds, unless they are very old, seldom need to have toenails cut: but cage pets almost invariably need to have them attended to by the time they are adult, sometimes earlier. The reason is that they cannot 'file down', their claws by contact with hard rough surfaces such as paving stones, or the wire of the flight in which they are housed.

It is quite easy to cut the claws of a cockatiel if it is first wrapped securely in a towel. Allow the bird's head to be free so that it can breathe freely and also occupy itself with biting the towel, extract a leg, and with the aid of a torch look for the 'quick' in each claw, give a good clearance, and if in doubt, leave that claw alone. A blood vessel which is cut will give the bird a sharp stinging pain, and if the bleeding is not stopped the bird could bleed to death. A sharp pair of nail scissors, or the special cutters for dog's toenails, obtainable from veterinary establishments, will do the job very well. Some cockatiels have dark toenails or claws, making it impossible to see the 'quick'; these are best filed a little rather than cut. It will be necessary to use a metal file.

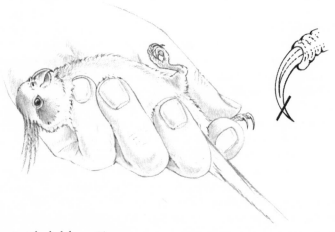

Correct method of claw cutting.

HOSPITAL CAGES

There are many types of commercially-built hospital cages available. Most have underfloor heat, and a thermometer above, which does not necessarily give the temperature of the *floor*, and that is where most really ill birds are likely to find themselves. An egg-bound hen can suffer acute discomfort from too hot a floor, the double shock of egg-binding and too much heat can cause death.

If a hospital cage with underfloor heat is used, be sure to put a thermometer on the *floor* of the cage, so that the correct temperature can be maintained at floor level.

A very useful substitute for a hospital cage can be arranged by simply putting the bird in an ordinary single breeder cage, this means a cage with wooden top and three wooden sides, leaving the front only with wire.

Such a cage can be placed near a radiator, or in front of a small electric fire; or better still, a heat lamp can be placed near the front of the cage. The bird will benefit greatly if the heat lamp is a kind which emits infra-red rays.

STRESS, CHILDREN AND ILL BIRDS

Children should never be allowed near ill birds; both for their own health and that of the birds. A bird which may appear to be suffering from nothing more than a chill, due to cold weather, or a strained eye due to dust, may a few days later develop a much more serious illness.

For the above reasons it is always better to exclude children from an area used for an ill or indisposed bird. Dogs and cats play a large part in stressing birds, although I have never yet met a cat owner who would believe that *their* pussy stressed their birds.

Stress is not always obvious, but it plays such a large part in the development of illness in birds that it cannot be emphasised too strongly; ill birds in particular, should *never* be subjected to the sort of stress which can be produced by the presence of young children, dogs, and cats.

The above advice does not mean that the bird should be shut away on its own: the sights and sounds of a normal household, and the encouragement of its owner's voice will aid its fight to recover enormously.

GIVING MEDICINE TO COCKATIELS

How to give medicine to birds is a question that seems to puzzle a lot of people. It should be remembered that putting medicine in the drinking water, or sprinkling powder on to seeds or soft food is a very hit and miss method of dealing with illness.

Cockatiels, like many other Australian birds, can easily go without water for two days if they consider they must, and could

99

probably do so for longer. Since antibiotics are normally given for five days, with a five day rest, this would then throw the whole medication programme out of balance.

It is much better to give any medicine over the tongue, with the aid of a hypodermic syringe which has had its needle removed.

As already discussed, when the medicine to be given is an antibiotic it is very necessary to give the bird a *daily* dose of pure, plain yoghourt two hours before the antibiotic dose. Once per day will be sufficient, and two beakfuls is quite enough; it is best to do this with a syringe.

Birds, especially ill ones, very quickly get used to being given medicine with a syringe, eye dropper, or even a small spoon. It is very noticeable that as soon as a medicine starts to work, and the bird concerned begins to feel better, it is inordinately thankful to its owner, and excited at the prospect of fresh life.

Cockatiels are very intelligent little birds, and know very well when something is doing them good. Medicine which does no good after five days of medication may not be suiting the bird. When a bird fails to rally at all, it would be best to ask the advice of the veterinarian as to whether another type of medicine could be tried. He or she should be consulted immediately if the bird seems to be going 'downhill' at any stage in its medication.

INTERNAL BLEEDING FROM WOOD CHIPS
It is unusual for cockatiels to eat so much wood that they bleed from the intestines, but it could happen with a bored pet cockatiel. In this case the bird should be given a dose of liquid medicinal paraffin, one teaspoonful of which should be sufficient to clear out any sharp bits of wood.

A branch of willow, apple, or beech, stripped of the leaves but not the tiny buds, would provide the bird with a more digestible and enjoyable kind of wood to chew than its own perch.

EXCRETA
Many newcomers to cockatiels tend to get very worried if the colour of their bird's excreta alters. The normal healthy colour is black or very dark green and white; the white is the urine. Much anxiety could be saved if it is realised that bird's droppings alter according to the weather, the food they are receiving, and whether or not they are stressed.

Bright yellow may indicate some disease, but is is just as likely that it indicates that it has been a cold day and the birds have been sitting out in the wind.

Bright green may indicate illness, but it will also occur if the birds gorge themselves on dark green cabbage, lettuce, etc.

Completely liquid droppings may indicate something wrong with the birds, but they can also be the result of temporary stress. Before rushing off to the veterinarian, look at the birds' eyes and vents. If the birds are normal and bright eyed when disturbed slightly, and if the vents are clean and dry, leave them alone and wait to see if the droppings return to normal in a day or two.

SWOLLEN EYES

One of the commonest afflictions to beset cockatiels, especially red-eyed ones such as lutinos, lutino pearls, silvers, fallows and albinos, is eye strain. This is often no more than dust in the eye, then the bird rubs the eye on the perch, and soon it is swollen and sore.

Bathe the eye with warm water and, with a soft cloth, brush any feathers well away from the eyes. If the swelling continues after two days of twice daily bathing, take the bird to a veterinarian who will probably prescribe an antibiotic eye-cream. A tiny 'worm' shaped bit of this should be gently squeezed on to the lower lid of the eye.

Always bathe a swollen eye with lukewarm water and a soft cloth or handkerchief, *not* cotton wool. Tiny threads of the cotton wool can get into the eye, and do more harm than good.

Eyes should always be bathed just before an application of any kind of external medicine. In the case of an antibiotic cream it is usual to give it for five days, then give a five day rest, with a daily or twice daily application of a bland cream, then another five days of the antibiotic cream.

If the eyes are not cured by this time the swollen area is probably indicative of some internal complaint.

BROKEN TAIL FEATHERS

Some birds, especially young ones, suffer from a condition in which their tail feathers constantly break. Often the sheath remains on the feather, failing to break away to release the growing feather. The reason for this is not certain; it could be feather mites, or possibly the result of weakness caused by inbreeding.

These birds can be greatly helped by being given a bath in the very excellent disinfectant for kennels and livestock known Vanodine V18® (made by Vanodine International, Bamber Bridge, Preston, Lancs., England).

A bath of lukewarm water should be coloured deep golden brown with Vanodine®. The bird should be stood in the bath and the water poured over the bird many times and gently massaged into the skin above and below the tail, until it is totally soaked with the water and disinfectant.

The bird should then be wrapped in a dry towel to remove as much liquid as possible, and put in a clean warm cage to dry out in a warm room. Two or three baths at intervals of one week may be necessary if the tail feather loss is severe.

11 Diseases and Veterinary Care

By Alan Jones B. Vet. Med., MRCVS

In general, cockatiels are hardy and easily kept birds, but they do have their disease problems. Illness in most birds is outwardly rapid when it does occur, and often the first sign of trouble noticed by an owner is a dead bird on the floor of the cage or aviary. This is because *acute* infections progress quickly because of the bird's rapid metabolic rate, and a very short period of lack of appetite or fever will weaken a bird drastically. Conversely *chronic* low-grade infections can fester within a bird for a very long time before they produce sufficient damage to weaken a bird, which will then suddenly deteriorate as if only just taken ill.

A bird keeper who gets to know his birds will recognise slight differences in behaviour or attitude which could indicate early disease problems before they become too advanced, and therefore regular inspection is important. The quick visit to the aviary to push in food and water will be of no use since most birds will look bright and alert when suddenly disturbed: one must observe the birds quietly and over a period of time to spot any that are behaving oddly.

The time factor is so critical to save a sick bird by seeking knowledgeable veterinary attention that the observant owner who has some basic understanding of the likely disease problems will have a great advantage, and that is the purpose of this chapter

To understand what happens in a sick bird a little knowledge of basic anatomy and physiology of the cockatiel is essential. The cockatiel is classified in the animal kingdom as follows:

Class AVES
Order PSITTACIFORMES
Family PSITTACIDAE
Sub-Family CACATUINAE (COCKATOOS)
Species *Nymphicus hollandicus*

However in many ways of form and behaviour the cockatiel resembles the grass parakeet. Its familiar streamlined shape, with long wings and tail, perch-adapted feet, and decorative crest contrast with the squatter body, rounded wings, short fan-like tail, climbing feet and crest actively used in display of the archetypal cockatoos.

Birds are homoeothermic or warm-blooded, a character shared with the mammals. This means that they have a high body temperature which is strictly regulated from within by various

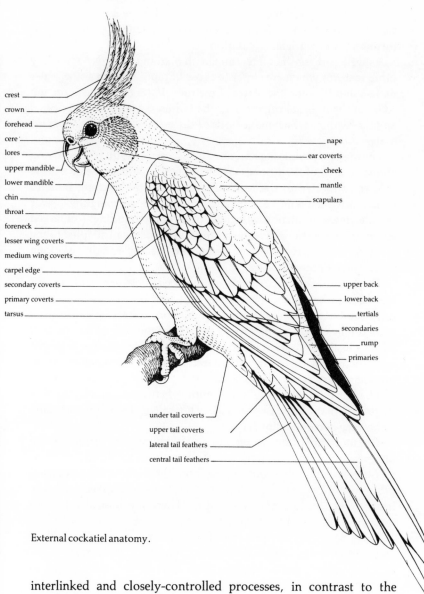

crest
crown
forehead
cere
lores
upper mandible
lower mandible
chin
throat
foreneck
lesser wing coverts
medium wing coverts
carpel edge
secondary coverts
primary coverts
tarsus

nape
ear coverts
cheek
mantle
scapulars

upper back
lower back
tertials
secondaries
rump
primaries

under tail coverts
upper tail coverts
lateral tail feathers
central tail feathers

External cockatiel anatomy.

interlinked and closely-controlled processes, in contrast to the poikilothermic or cold-blooded reptiles, fish, and amphibians, whose body temperature is affected by their environment. This means that when the bird's environment is hotter than its body it has to lose heat, which it does by panting, seeking shade, bathing, and spreading its feathers to allow air to circulate over the skin. Most of the time, however, the reverse is true and the bird needs to maintain a temperature higher than that of its surroundings. The colder the outside temperature, the more work has to be done to achieve this state, by increasing food intake to provide more metabolisable

103

energy, by exercising to produce muscular heat, by huddling together to conserve warmth, and by reducing the blood flow through the superficial circulation.

As well as these shared features with mammals, birds have many other features which are closer to those of reptiles, such as the scales on feet and legs and the claws of the toes. Parts of the skeleton and some of the internal organs (e.g. the kidneys) are reptilian in type, and the feathers which make birds so distinctive are in fact modified scales

The major adaptations unique to birds are the result of their flying ability – most of their bones are strong but light because of hollow centres connected to the respiratory system; the pectoral muscles which move the wings are massively enlarged, forming the 'breast muscle' mass, which is attached to a correspondingly enlarged sternum, or keel bone. The respiratory system is well adapted to the massive oxygen requirement demanded by the rapidly working muscles when the bird flies.

There are several major differences between avian and mammalian anatomy. The larynx is small, and has a protective function, but has no use in voice production. Instead, birds have an extra organ known as the syrinx, situated at the *base* of the trachea, where most vocalisation is produced. Considering the fairly simple construction of this organ compared with the mammalian voice-producing larynx plus the fact that the latter animals make great use of changing the shape of the mouth when communicating, it is surprising that birds can produce such a range of sounds, including some very accurate mimicry.

The most important difference in the respiratory system is the presence of air sacs. The lungs are comparatively small, and are fixed and barely expansible, but arising from them and their associated tubing are several air sacs, which are thin-walled, usually transparent, membranous envelopes. There are basically 12, but these may be joined or modified in different species.

These sacs have some function in gas exchange through their walls, some function in warming and humidifying the inspired air, and the interclavicular sac can be massively inflated for use in courtship display in some species such as frigate birds and pouter pigeons. The sacs also increase the buoyancy of the body. They communicate with hollow cavities in many of the long bones, which is an important consideration because of infections; but their primary purpose is to act as bellows to move air into and out of the lungs. There is no muscular diaphragm which in mammals performs most of this task, and thus there is direct communication between

Avian digestive tract and alimentary canal (by Ray Hutchins).

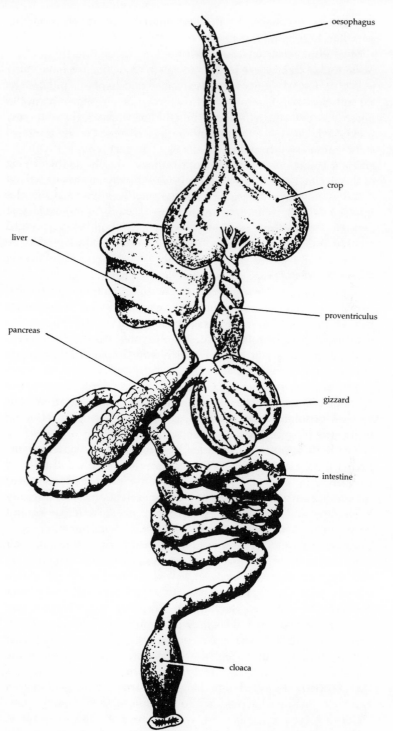

oesophagus

crop

liver

proventriculus

pancreas

gizzard

intestine

cloaca

105

the thorax and abdomen, another important point when dealing with infectious conditions.

Most inspired air is drawn past the lung tissue directly into the posterior air sacs, where some is retained, while the remainder then passes through the lungs for gas exchange to take place, and on into the anterior sacs. Expiratory action forces the air remaining in the posterior sacs through the lungs, into the anterior sacs, from where it is expelled. There is a fairly continuous movement of air – and no static pause as is found in mammals. This fact, coupled with the efficient absorption mechanism of the lungs, plus the double-action of the air flow, means that oxygen is very rapidly absorbed into the blood stream. For the same reasons, anything contained in the inspired air such as an anaesthetic or irritant gas, or fungal spores and micro-organisms, is rapidly dispersed through the system and quickly absorbed.

The major features of the bird's digestive tract differing from mammals are the crop, the stomach, and the cloaca. the former is a diverticulum of the oesophagus, and acts as a temporary reservoir for food, as well as a feeding bottle for nestling chicks, The stomach is divided into two chambers: the first is the glandular pro-ventriculus, which produces digestive enzymes; from there the food passes to the muscular gizzard, which with the aid of ingested grit grinds up the hard seeds.

The large intestine and the ureters from the kidneys open into a common chamber known as the cloaca, so that waste from both systems is combined and voided together through the vent. Thus the bird's dropping consists of a semi-solid faecal portion, which is normally dark green, surrounded by a white urinary component. Since the cockatiel originates from a naturally arid area and eats a basically dry diet, its normal droppings are small and dry, contrasting with the very wet and bulky excreta of a fruit eater.

The heart and circulatory system of the cockatiel is fundamentally very similar to that of mammals, with two noteworthy exceptions. The red blood cells (erythrocytes) retain their nuclei in birds, and are more oval in shape than those of mammals. Secondly, there is a renal portal system found in birds as well as the hepatic portal system found in both groups. That is to say that some blood returning from the legs passes through the kidneys before reaching the heart and becoming re-circulated. This may be significant if giving drugs by injection into the leg. The hepatic portal system involves the passage of blood from the gut through the liver before its return to the heart.

Having briefly described something of the structures of the cockatiel and their functions I should like to mention some of the important factors involved in the diagnosis and treatment of a disease problem.

If you are to take a sick bird to veterinary surgeon, there is a certain amount of information that he or she will need in order to make a diagnosis. There is often little difference in the outward signs of illness in birds, although they may be ill from a wide variety of diseases – that is to say that a sick bird looks miserable, fluffed up and quiet, probably not eating, and usually with loose droppings, but it could have any of a dozen complaints. Therefore careful questioning and detailed background information is important before we even look at the bird, in order that we can get some clues to the disease involved.

Where possible, the veterinarian will prefer to examine the patient at the surgery (office), where there are more complete facilities for diagnosis and treatment, but on occasions it can be an advantage to see the bird in its own environment, especially when several birds are involved.

Having decided to take your bird to the surgery, the following points should be considered.

1) Ideally, bring in the bird's own cage. In the case of larger species or aviary birds, this may not be possible, in which case a transport cage or box must be used, but certain information can be gained from seeing the bird's normal accommodation.

2) Cover the cage and warm the car before the journey.

3) Remove water, to avoid spillage, but bring the bird's food for inspection, plus any medication already given. Owners will often try a remedy on the advice of a friend or pet-shop before seeking veterinary attention, and it is helpful to be able to see what has already been used, before administering any more drugs.

4) Do *not* remove the droppings, or try to clean the cage. One can well appreciate the wish of the owner to assure the veterinarian that his/her bird is hygienically looked after, but if the cage is scrubbed and presented in pristine condition, any information such as the appearance and quantity of droppings, the possibilities of blood or vomit, and other things such as the presence of mites in crevices of the cage will have been eliminated.

The veterinary surgeon should then ask such questions as:

1) What is the presenting problem, and how long has it been observed? How frequently do signs occur, or are they present all the time?

2) How long has the bird been owned, and where did it come from?

3) Is this the only bird affected, or are there others? If so, how many, and what species?

4) Have there been any previous illnesses, and what treatments were given?

5) Does the bird stay in its cage permanently, or is it allowed to fly free? If so, is there any history of flying into obstacles in the home? Can it reach and eat houseplants or wallpaper?

6) Has there been any recent change in the environment of the bird – has it been moved to a new room, or even across the same room; has there been any building or decorating going on, or treatments such as dry rot or woodworm; has there been a change of household routine such as visitors staying; or any accidents such as fires or chemical spillage occurring?

7) Has there been any change in feeding routine or food type and source of supply? If so, how long ago? If possible, bring samples of both new and old food for checking. New fruits or vegetables are often given when in season, but the bird may not be used to them. Has he been given branches or twigs from unsuitable trees to chew?

The veterinarian can then proceed to look at the bird itself. He should first observe it quietly, watching attitude and position, looking for signs of wheezing or tail bobbing, and noting its interest or otherwise in its surroundings.

Only then should he hold and examine the bird in more detail, being especially careful, of course, if signs of respiratory distress have already been observed, as handling such a bird can be fatal. A very nervous bird is best approached by lowering the lighting, and ensuring a quiet, calm attitude. A tame cockatiel can be held in a bare hand, but it can inflict a painful bite if frightened, so if in doubt it is best to use a small towel for protection. The bird is cupped in the hand, with the first two fingers on either side of the head, the thumb supporting one wing, and the third and fourth fingers holding the other wing closed to the body. The other hand is then free to examine the bird, or ideally an experienced assistant can hold the bird in this way, allowing the veterinarian both hands free. One must be aware of how much pressure is being put on the bird: it needs to be held firmly but gently, so that it is restrained but comfortable, and therefore confident. It should not be squeezed so tightly that it cannot breathe.

Hopefully, having come this far, the veterinary surgeon can make a tentative diagnosis and initiate suitable treatment, but often further information will be required, which will necessitate hospitalisation and perhaps X-ray examination, or laboratory tests on blood or droppings.

The importance of post mortem examination (autopsy) must be

mentioned here. Obviously the examination of a dead single pet bird serves no great advantage to the owner except to prove a diagnosis or satisfy curiosity; but where several birds are kept together, useful information can be gained which could save the lives of surviving birds. It can even be worth sacrificing a very sick bird that probably will not live, in order that a specific diagnosis may be made at *post mortem*, and the rest of the flock at risk can then be successfully treated before they too succumb. A single bird found suddenly dead may well have died from an individual problem such as a heart attack or accident, but it could equally be the first affected by a contagious disease, and only autopsy will distinguish that fact.

We can now proceed to consider some of the more specific disease problems afflicting cockatiels. The important points to emphasise in treating any sick bird are *speed, warmth,* and *fluids.* As mentioned earlier a bird will weaken very rapidly when ill, and therefore regular inspection of the stock with prompt treatment where indicated will save lives. It is no good thinking 'he looks a bit rough tonight. I'll check him again in the morning', because tomorrow is likely to be too late.

Having identified a potential patient, the next stage is to provide isolation and warmth. Many a sick bird can be saved by increased temperature alone, without recourse to drug treatment. The ideal is a small cage and an infra-red heat lamp, which can be mounted to one side. The bird is then able to move to the other side of the cage if it gets too hot. Failing this, local heat can be provided with a low wattage light bulb, or else the whole room must be heated to *at least* 70°F, or preferably 75-80°F. The cage can be shielded with a blanket or thick towel. Once the bird has recovered, it is important to lower the temperature again gradually, and not put him straight back outside into a cold aviary.

Thirdly, a sick bird will dehydrate rapidly, especially if feverish, diarrhoeic, or vomiting. It can survive without food for a little while, but must be made to drink. Water is best boiled, and offered not too cold, and is more effective with the addition of a little honey, glucose, or brown sugar. Once under the heat lamp, the patient is likely to drink readily, but if not, the liquid must be given by hand, using a dropper, syringe, or small spoon. Try to get him to take a few drops every 30-40 minutes.

These three steps, with nursing and 'TLC' (tender loving care) will save many a bird.

ACCIDENTS
Cockatiels are swift and fairly skilful fliers, but many accident cases are a result of their flying into obstacles in the aviary or home, especially when frightened. They may also be injured by other birds

or animals. Much of this subject has been covered in the chapter on first aid, and most bruising or grazing injuries are simply dealt with by antiseptic bathing and perhaps some antibiotic dusting powder. Birds that fly into windows or mirrors can haemorrhage from the beak. This may be stemmed in the same way as bleeding from careless beak or nail-clipping with a styptic pencil, a little ferrous sulphate or potassium permanganate, or even just finger pressure over a little dry cotton wool.

If a beak injury is severe, the beak base may start to separate after a few days. The damaged layers will peel off, and new beak tissue will regrow but the bird will need a soft food diet or even hand-feeding for a while. Such a bird must also be checked for signs of concussion or skull damage.

Broken bones in wings or legs are common accident problems, and once the bird has been treated as described in the chapter on first aid, the injury is best inspected by a veterinarian.

Broken bones heal very rapidly in birds, but if a successful return to normal function is to be achieved it is important to ensure that the broken fragments are aligned and apposed accurately. Because of the comparatively light bodyweight and delicate structure of a bird, heavy splints, strappings, or plaster casts are unsuccessful. Any method used to support the bones must be light but strong, and must not be left in place for too long, or else muscle wastage, tendon contracture, and joint fixation will occur, which may cripple the bird more severely than the original fracture.

Internal fixation of broken leg bones by intramedullary pinning is successfully employed in larger parrots and raptors, but for birds the size of a cockatiel it is rarely necessary to resort to such surgery. Most leg or wing fractures will heal adequately with simple strapping as described below, and although return to normal function may be less than 100 per cent, this is seldom of serious importance in the cage or aviary cockatiel.

Leg fractures are best supported with adhesive tape or plaster placed on either side of the limb, with the bird held on its back and the leg extended. Once the bones are re-aligned and the joints are in as near normal an angle of flexion as possible for perching, the plaster is secured on each side, with an overlap to front and back of the leg. This overlap can then be 'crimped' with artery forceps (haemostats) to secure the support.

Broken wings are supported by holding the wings in their normal resting flexed position, then fixing them in place with a tape encircling the shoulder area. A small tape is wrapped around the wing tips at their crossover, to provide further support and counter-balance, and in larger birds a third tape may be laid longitudinally to join the first two. A suitable tape for this technique is masking or autoclave tape, which is light but strong and will stay attached for the duration of healing, but is much more easily removed from the feathers when the time comes than is either Sellotape® or adhesive plaster.

Most fractures should be well healed by 3-4 weeks, but it is worth checking and replacing the strapping at 10-14 days. The bird should be kept cage-confined for a further 2 weeks after the support is finally removed.

TIGHT RINGS

Many individual birds will have leg rings of plastic or metal which can cut into the leg and cause circulatory problems if they are too tight, or the foot becomes swollen. These must be rapidly removed by a veterinary surgeon, otherwise the foot will die because of lack of blood supply. Plastic rings are fairly easily cut, but aluminium types require a little more care and effort. They may cut by nibbling action with the tips of open-ended nail clippers, or there is a specific ring-removing tool available, which has a scissor action, and a fine lower blade which should insert under the ring.

WING, BEAK & NAIL CLIPPING

Beak trimming is rarely necessary in cockatiels, compared to the frequent problem encountered in budgerigars, but if one half of the beak gets damaged the opposite half may require regular attention. Likewise nails rarely over-grow in aviary birds, with sufficient exercise and varied sized branches for perching, but cage pets often need their nails trimmed. Both beak and claws can be cut with care using a small nail-clipper or stout blunt-ended scissors. The 'quick' or vein is usually visible in lighter coloured individuals but if cut the haemorrhage is readily controlled with a styptic, ferrous sulphate, potassium permanganate, or cotton wool pressure as mentioned above.

It can be an advantage to trim the wings of indoor pet cockatiels, to prevent them flying into windows and ornaments, but make sure they are not so incapacitated that they cannot escape the family cat or dog! The procedure involves cutting the primary feathers on *one* wing so that the bird is unbalanced and cannot gain lift. A bird with *both* wings trimmed can remain balanced and can often get enough lift to fly using just the secondaries.

The cosmetic technique used with some birds retains the first 2 primary feathers while the next 6-8 are cut across using a sharp pair of straight scissors at the level of the tips of the secondaries. This is done looking at the *outer* surface of the wing, and *not* at the inner level of secondaries. This method results in a neat appearance when the bird is at rest with its wings crossed, but is rarely successful in cockatiels, because they are such strong fliers that they can manage on just the remaining 2 flight feathers. It is far better to cut all the first 8-10 primaries.

111

SKIN & FEATHER CONDITIONS

Traumatic skin lesions have been mentioned under the chapter on first aid and accidents; cockatiels are rarely affected by other skin problems. Occasionally, ulcers and scabs resulting from avian pox or bacterial dermatitis may be seen – these are best treated with local antiseptic or antibacterial preparations.

Skin tumours, both benign and malignant, are common findings on budgerigars, but are infrequently encountered in cockatiels. Occasionally *feather cysts* are seen, where a feather fails to erupt normally through the skin and grows as a curled-up deformed mass within the follicle, gradually accumulating a caseous debris, which is irritating to the bird, and is best excised. This is usually a fairly simple technique which may not even require local anaesthesia, but feather cysts are well supplied with blood vessels, and haemostasis is important.

There is some evidence that the tendency to feather cysts is inherited; and that they may also be associated with hypothyroidism.

The uropygial, or preen gland, located above the base of the tail, is an organ producing essential oils and waxes which the bird spreads over its feathers while preening. This can sometimes be the site of abscesses or tumours, which again may be surgically excised.

Deficiencies of various minerals, vitamins or amino acids in the diet may occasionally affect feather appearance. Choline and riboflavin deficiencies result in loss of pigmentation; lack of pantothenic acid prevents growth of body feathers; and absence of lysine produces poor feather development, but without the diagnostic white patches seen in other avian species.

FEATHER PLUCKING

This is a commonly encountered problem, and may be a result of an attack by other dominant birds in the colony (even parents to their chicks) in which case the head and neck are most usually affected. Self-inflicted plucking manifests as loss and damage of body feathers, and in the absence of parasitic or irritant disease is most often the result of boredom, inactivity, or environmental stress and will progress to a habit which becomes difficult to break.

Attention to diet, hygiene, temperature, humidity, and 'occupational therapy' are all important, and in extreme cases an Elizabethan collar may be employed to prevent the bird self-mutilating. In the USA the majority of feather plucking cockatiels prove to be infected with giardiasis, an intestinal protozoan parasite which seems to provoke severe pruritus. This is not a problem commonly encountered in the UK.

Other cases of feather plucking are hormonal in origin, occurring in hyper-sexed frustrated individuals, and if all other methods of control fail may be treated by the judicious use of progesterone.

French moult may be encountered in cockatiels, but is more of a problem in budgerigars and lovebirds. The long feathers of tail and wings are lost or deformed, and the problem becomes progressively more evident in broods hatched later in the year. The aetiology of the condition is still not fully understood, but there is evidence that there may be viral infection coupled with an inherited predisposition.

EXTERNAL PARASITES

These do not cause severe problems in cockatiels, although mosquitoes or gnats may be a source of irritation to nesting birds in warm weather, and may also be vectors of blood protozoic diseases.

Harvest mites or forage mites can cause some degree of skin irritation and fleas, bugs, or ticks are occasionally encountered. All these are easily eliminated with the use of insecticidal sprays or powders containing pyrethrins (e.g. Willothrin®) or bromocyclen (e.g. Alugan® – Hoechst), and attention to hygiene in the crevices of cages or nest boxes.

Feather lice can be more troublesome, producing signs of restlessness, ruffled appearance, and continual preening. These parasites are large enough to be seen with the naked eye, and their eggs are visible stuck alongside the feather shafts. Since their whole life cycle is spent on the bird, they are readily eliminated by the regular use of the above parasiticides at 7-10 day intervals.

'Scaly face' or 'scaly leg' caused by the burrowing mite *Cnemidocoptes pilae* is nowhere near as commonly found in cockatiels as it is in budgerigars, and can be treated with local application of substances such as benzyl benzoate or Dettol®, although more recently a single treatment with one injection of Ivermectin® at the required dilution has proved highly effective.

Surface dwelling mites such as *Dermanyssus gallinae* (red mite) can be a serious irritant to birds, and in sufficient numbers can result in debility and anaemia because of their blood-sucking activities. They can also transmit blood protozoa such as *Lankesterella*. These red mites live in cracks and crevices in the environment, and only come out to feed on the birds at night, so they are best detected at this time by covering the cage or nest box with a white cloth, on which the parasites will collect and be visible as red dots after their blood meal. Treatment and elimination depends more on scrubbing the environment, using washing soda followed by an insecticide such as Malathion®, rather than treating the birds directly.

CONJUNCTIVITIS

Inflamed and infected eyes are commonly encountered in cockatiels, and may be part of a more generalised respiratory infection (see below), but are more often primary conditions in their own right. Conjunctivitis (inflammation of the membranes of the eye) and blepharitis (swelling and inflammation of the eyelid) may result from irritants such as a cold draught, disinfectant, pieces of sand and grit, or attack from other birds. These causes are best treated as described in the chapter on first aid, by bathing and perhaps a bland ophthalmic ointment. Red-eyed, light coloured birds seem particularly susceptible.

Infectious conjunctivitis is caused by a variety of organisms, perhaps the most persistent of which is *Mycoplasma*. Elimination of this organism requires prolonged use of a suitable antibiotic preparation (ideally selected as a result of culture and sensitivity testing of the organism) maintained for 3-4 weeks. Preparations in the form of drops are usually easier to apply than ointments, but the latter have the advantage of a more lasting effect on the eye. As with ophthalmic problems in any animal, where there is ulceration of the corneal surface, preparations containing corticosteroid should not be used; the protective technique of suturing the eyelids over in these cases is perfectly feasible in cockatiels.

One should always look for signs of associated diseases when a bird with conjunctivitis is presented, as this condition is often connected with sinusitis or other respiratory tract diseases.

FROST-BITE
This can be a real problem in aviary birds perching in severe weather, as the toes are very small, with no feather protection and a limited blood supply, and are therefore easily affected by sub-zero temperatures. Affected toes will become dark in colour, shrivel and become stiff, and are best amputated, although they will eventually drop off if left untreated.

CONDITIONS AFFECTING THE RESPIRATORY SYSTEM

SINUSITIS
This is a very common ailment in many of the larger psittacine birds, but as has already been stated the cockatiel is a generally hardy bird and is not afflicted by disease problems to the same degree. However, sinusitis does occur, and can be just as persistent and difficult to cure as in the larger birds.

As mentioned in the description of the respiratory system, the bird has many air sacs which intercommunicate and also connect with the sinuses, which are air chambers within the bones of the skull. These chambers can become a site of chronic infection, occasionally as the result of injury, but usually in association with respiratory infection. There are many organisms involved, including Mycoplasmas, and often several bacteria are present in combination. Progress of the condition is slow, and the pus which gradually accumulates tends to

114

be thick and caseous, therefore by the time signs are noticed, treatment with systemic antibiotics alone is rarely successful in penetrating and dispersing the infection.

Affected birds have swelling above or below one or both eyes, with resulting closure of the palpebral fissure, and sometimes swelling is evident between the rami of the mandible. If the swelling is soft, the pus may be extracted by needle puncture and suction with a syringe. The sinus can then be irrigated with an antiseptic or antibiotic solution via the needle, or via the nostril. This procedure often needs repeating until full resolution is achieved. If, however, the swelling is firm because the content is caseous, then surgical removal of the plug is necessary using a fine pointed scalpel blade, again followed by antibiotic lavage. Commonly indicated antibiotics are Tylosin, Gentamycin, or Lincomycin.

Birds have a very high requirement for vitamin A, and deficiency of this vitamin is very common, especially in birds fed a diet high in sunflower seed. Lack of the vitamin damages epithelial surfaces as mentioned below, and therefore allows secondary infections to gain access. Sinusitis is often associated with mild hypovitaminosis A, and any bird suffering from chronic respiratory disease will benefit from vitamin A therapy.

AVIAN POX

A common problem in many of the larger imported psittacines, especially Amazons, this condition can sometimes affect cockatiels. It starts with a watery eye and excessive blinking, progressing rapidly to marked blepharitis and conjunctivitis with considerable caseous exudate accumulating in the eyes. Birds become miserable, ruffled and inappetant, and usually snuffly and wheezy, with copious nasal discharge, as the infection invades the sinuses and air sacs. Scabby pox lesions then appear around the eyelids and face, and sometimes elsewhere on the body, and in a recovered bird they can result in considerable damage and distortion of the eyelids.

Treatment is non-specific and supportive, including isolation of infected birds, with attention to hygiene and disinfection of cages and food bowls; increased warmth and humidity; careful regular bathing of nostrils and eyes to prevent sticky accumulations; and dressing of the eyes with a suitable antibiotic ointment. Enforced inhalation of decongestant vapours by placing a little Vick® or friars balsam in boiling water adjacent to a covered cage can be beneficial, and the offering of tempting food or even hand-feeding may be necessary. Drinking water can be enriched with glucose, honey, or fruit juices, and the addition of Chlorhexidine to the water at the rate of 10ml per gallon appears to reduce the spread of the virus.

Broad spectrum antiobiosis to reduce secondary infection is usually worthwhile, as is multi-vitamin therapy.

AIR SACCULITIS

This is a common disease entity in all birds, since for reasons mentioned in the description of the respiratory tract the air sacs are vulnerable to invasion and damage by a wide variety of pathogens.

Many cases of inflammation and resulting exudate are caused by irritant vapours such as ammonia, coal tar disinfectants, lime, and paraffin (kerosene). A particular hazard is the vapour given off by overheating saucepans coated with certain non-stick polytetrafluoroethylene (PTFE) preparations, which is extremely noxious to humans, and rapidly fatal to birds.

Infectious agents include viruses such as Newcastle Disease and Avian Pox, bacteria such as *E.coli*, streptococcus, *Pasteurella*, *Yersinia*, *Klebsiella*, *Salmonella*, *Mycobacterium tuberculosis*, Mycoplasma and Chlamydia, and fungal agents such as *Aspergillus*. Acute cases manifest with signs of depression, lack of appetite, and the general misery of any sick bird, but with the added indicators of a nasal discharge and tail bobbing. Most birds flick their tails repeatedly when excited or alarmed, but the motion ceases on relaxation. A bird that is suffering from respiratory disease – either sacculitis or pneumonia – will continue to tail bob when at rest. Auscultation with a stethoscope will reveal bubbly fluid or wheezy sounds.

Treatment is along the same lines as those described for pox, with attention to nursing and symptomatic relief, plus the use of a broad spectrum antibiotic such as Tylosin, Chloromycetin, or Chlortetracycline.

Chronic forms, usually associated with tuberculosis or aspergillosis, appear as longer lasting debility, with marked loss of weight, and dry rasping sounds on auscultation. There may be an audible 'click' as pieces of dried exudate are moved in the sacs by the flow of air. Such cases are difficult to diagnose in life, and almost impossible to cure.

Aspergillus fumigatus is a ubiquitous fungus whose spores can be inhaled to develop an infection within the respiratory system. The spores germinate and grow into a mould mass on the lining membranes, accumulating a caseous exudate in the process. Birds are more susceptible to infection if already debilitated, and spores are then readily contracted from damp, rotting fruit or vegetables. Attention must be paid therefore to the general condition of birds and their feeding to avoid the development of this distressing and virtually incurable disease. Any wasted fruit or seed should be rapidly cleared away. If seed is purchased in bulk before feeding, it should be stored in cool, dry, dark conditions, which will delay the development of mould formation, and also reduce the rate of loss of vitamin activity. Warm, damp, light situations have the opposite, undesirable effect.

PNEUMONIA

This is an acute, often per-acute, infection of the lungs, by any of the bacteria or viruses mentioned above, and can be rapidly fatal. Signs seen are those described for sacculitis, including tail bobbing, but are usually more rapid in onset and more marked, and without the nasal discharge. Auscultation of the thorax reveals moist râles.

Supportive treatment with heat and fluid therapy is vitally important, as is rapid antibiotic therapy. Oral administration in food or drinking water is unlikely to be effective quickly enough, and the bird will probably not take it voluntarily anyway. This is one occasion when direct oral administration by dropper, or better still intramuscular injection, is positively indicated. Both methods involve handling and severely stressing a very sick bird, and this can prove fatal, but without the treatment a bird with pneumonia will usually die anyway.

PSITTACOSIS

This important disease features respiratory as well as enteric signs, which brings us on to the next section of illness, but it is worthy of a little consideration by itself.

The causal organism is *Chlamydia psittaci*, an agent which is like a virus in that it can only grow and multiply within the cells of its host animal, but in other ways is like a bacterium, including being susceptible to antibiotics, especially tetracyclines. It is a ubiquitous organism, and affects many species in a variety of ways, causing abortion in goats and sheep, conjunctivitis and respiratory disease in cats and dogs, severe respiratory disease in humans, and generalised illness with mainly respiratory signs in birds. The general condition is referred to as chlamydiosis in any species, ornithosis when it affects birds, and psittacosis when occurring specifically in psittacine birds. The latter is the name by which it is most familiar to aviculturists.

There are several strains of varying virulence, and the severity of the disease will depend on the pathogenicity of the strain, and the susceptibility of the host. Some species such as parakeets have a high innate resistance, whereas finches have very little resistance and therefore a high mortality rate.

The condition is complicated by the fact that numerous birds harbour the organism without showing any signs of illness – these are known as carriers. These individuals can start to excrete the organism and thus infect other birds if they are subject to stress such as import and quarantine, transportation, other disease, or change of routine. Thus the introduction of a new bird into an aviary can have dire consequences should it be carrying the infection.

The chlamydia are excreted from an infected bird in the faeces and nasal discharges, and transmission to other birds is by aerosol

117

formation and dust carried from the deposits. Incubation can vary from 4-100 days, however, so contact with an infected bird may have occurred long before the signs develop. The organism can survive for several months off the host in a dirty environment, but spread of infection is reduced by careful disposal of waste and seed, damping down floors, and daily disinfection. A good disinfectant is benzalkonium chloride.

Birds which contract the disease will show upper respiratory signs – i.e. conjunctivitis, discharge from the eyes and nose, blocked nostrils and snuffly breathing, plus listlessness and loss of appetite. There is usually a bright green diarrhoea, sometimes with blood staining. Long standing cases become very emaciated.

Positive diagnosis in life is difficult, and can only be performed in a specialist laboratory. Blood samples may be tested for antibodies to chlamydia, but to prove current infection compared to exposure sometime in the past, two samples are needed at 10-14 day intervals, showing a rising titre of antibodies. Faeces may be examined and cultured, but again this procedure takes 7-10 days, and samples must be very fresh for the organism to be found. Both techniques are therefore unable to give an immediate answer, but in the meantime steps must be taken to control the spread of suspected infection.

Post mortem diagnosis is more reliable and immediate; but should be carried out with care to prevent spread of infection to humans. Typical gross abnormalities include clouding of the air sacs, with variable amounts of exudation; enlargement and congestion of the liver; and gross enlargement of the spleen. All these signs may be seen in other septicaemic diseases, so are not in themselves conclusively diagnostic, but enlargement of the spleen particularly should always lead one to suspect psittacosis. This organ is situated underneath the gizzard, just to the left of the mid-line, and in a normal cockatiel would be perhaps 4-5mm in diameter. It is roughly spherical, and should be a rich red-brown in colour. A spleen infected with chlamydia enlarges to 3 or 4 times normal size, and may appear dark and congested, or mottled.

A more precise confirmation is achieved by taking impression smears from the cut surface of liver and spleen (and often air sac membrane and peritoneum). These are fixed and stained with a modified acid-fast technique; and microscopic examination will then reveal typical 'inclusion bodies' of chlamydia in infected cells. This procedure is fairly simple and quick and will give a 95 per cent confirmation of diagnosis. Final proof, however, depends on culturing the organism from the infected tissues, but this again takes time, and requires a very fresh carcase.

Apart from the problems that psittacosis causes in aviculture, a major consideration of this disease is that it is a zoonosis – that is to say that it is transmissible to humans and will produce a severe and unpleasant illness, which is occasionally fatal. Symptoms are basically 'flu-like' with chest pains and breathing difficulties, weakness, headaches and fevers. Any person showing such signs, especially if they appear not to clear up, and who has contact with birds, should always alert his medical doctor of the possibilities of psittacosis, which in the human case can be confirmed by a simple blood test. Treatment is usually rapidly successful with the use of tetracycline antibiotics.

Any bird-keeper and veterinarian faced with an outbreak of psittacosis has a difficult decision with regard to treatment and control. Spread of the disease within an avian population is rapid, mortality is high, and human contacts must be taken into consideration, especially where children or people with respiratory difficulties are involved. Slaughter of infected birds, followed by thorough disinfection should therefore be seriously considered as the right course of action.

Treatment is possible in selected cases, and should include isolation, thorough cleaning and disinfection, and the adminstration of chlortetracycline. This is best included in the feed, providing a more positive uptake than the common method of daily water medication, which allows rapid deterioration of the antibiotic. Severe, or single bird cases, may be treated by injectable tetracylines. In any event, the treatment *must* be substained for a minimum of 30, and preferably 45 days for any success to be achieved. The difficulties associated with the treatment of psittacosis are the variable and long incubation period, the prolonged medication required, the risk to humans involved during the process, and the fact that treated birds are immediately susceptible to reinfection once therapy ceases. Although measurable antibodies are produced in the blood, which can be used in diagnostic tests, these are not protective, and confer no immunity on the bird. Thus if the environment is still contaminated with organisms, the bird will immediately reinfect once antibiotic therapy ceases.

In the UK psittacosis is not a notifiable disease – i.e. public health authorities do not have to be involved in an outbreak, but any person connected with the infection in a bird should be aware of the potential serious damage to humans.

CONDITIONS AFFECTING THE ORAL CAVITY

Cockatiels are not seriously afflicted with disease problems in this region. Tumours are rare, unlike the fibrosarcoma problem of the budgerigar, or the papillomata of the macaws. Perhaps the three most likely conditions to be encountered are hypovitaminosis A (described later), trichomoniasis and candidiasis.

Trichomoniasis is most common in pigeons, where it is known as canker, and in raptors when it is called frounce. It is occasionally seen in finches, canaries and cockatiels. It is caused by a flagellate protozoan, in contrast to candidiasis, or thrush, which is the result of infection with a yeast organism. Both conditions have caseous deposits accumulating in the lining of the mouth and throat, and candidiasis more commonly extends down to the crop. Differentiation is simple by examination of a fresh smear under the microscope, looking for either motile flagellated trichomonads, or budding yeast cells of *Candida albicans*. Treatment of the former is usually effected with dimetridazole, and the latter with nystatin.

Candidiasis can occur in the crop, as can impaction with coarse material, or injuries and ulceration. These are not common in cockatiels, but are most likely to be seen in hand-reared youngsters as a result of feeding mixtures that are too hot and therefore scald the crop lining.

Primary diseases of proventriculus and gizzard are also rare: if these organs are affected it is usually as part of a more generalised condition.

LOOSE DROPPINGS

In the early part of this chapter it was pointed out that the droppings of a bird are a mix of both intestinal waste (faeces) and renal excretion (urine). The latter in birds is largely solid urate material, although there is a small proportion of actual liquid. The colour and appearance of the droppings produced can vary enormously even in one individual at different times and yet still be considered normal. The faecal content from a cockatiel is usually dark green, but will lighten if fruit or vegetable matter are consumed; the urine fraction is usually off-white. Droppings become more fluid if the bird is stressed or excited; those from egg-laying hens or from any bird first thing in the morning are much more copious than normal.

Loose droppings can be the result of an excessive fraction of urine – polyuria – and will be a reflection of kidney or liver disease; or it can be the result of excessive watery faeces — diarrhoea – originating from an enteric disturbance. It is important to differentiate which fraction of the droppings is affected in order to make the correct diagnosis and institute suitable treatment.

ENTERITIS (Inflammation of the bowel)

This can be caused by foreign irritants such as coarse diet, excessive grit, chemicals etc.; or by stress factors such as chilling, overcrowding, or change of diet; but most cases are infectious. Some viruses and fungi can be part of a more generalised disease such as psittacosis, but most cases of bowel inflammation are caused by worms (see below), protozoa, or bacteria.

Bacteria involved include *Pseudomonas, Pasteurella, Yersinia, Salmonella* commonly, and many others occasionally, but probably the most important is *Escherichia coli.* This is a ubiquitous bacterium, found in the gut of most mammals and carnivorous birds, but in common with other Gram-negative bacteria, is not normally found in seed and grain-eating birds such as the cockatiel. Infection is usually gained by contamination of food stuff by poor hygiene methods or from spoiling by rodents.

Affected birds will show the typical signs of illness – being ruffled, miserable, losing their appetite, etc., and passing liquid droppings of a pale colour. Specks of blood may be present. Treatment follows the usual course of isolation, warmth, oral fluids (if dehydration is sufficient, fluid therapy may be given by injection), soft food progressing to seed only, with the avoidance of fruit or green stuff, and antibiotic therapy, ideally as indicated by sensitivity testing.

Some cases may progress to a septicaemia – i.e. the *E.Coli* organism passes from the gut to invade the body as a whole, and such birds usually die. Post mortem examination reveals an enteritis, but also enlarged and congested liver, with cloudy air sacs and a greyish exudate on pericardial and air sac surfaces.

Of the protozoal infections causing enteritis, *Giardia intestinalis* is the most frequently encountered. It is an extremely common pathogen of cockatiels in the USA, but is not so regularly identified in Britain. It affects many other birds and mammals including man, and in the cockatiel produces a chronic or recurrent diarrhoea, which is bulky, foul smelling, and mucoid. The organism can be identified in fresh faecal smears examined microscopically, as an undulating, flagellated protozoan, and like trichomoniasis, may be treated with dimetridazole.

As mentioned in the section on feathers, infection of the gut with this parasite seems to provoke an intense pruritus in the skin, resulting in feather plucking. The exact connection is not clear: but any feather plucking cockatiel should be checked for the presence of giardia in the droppings.

INTERNAL PARASITES

Internal parasites are of prime importance in cockatiels – they include the roundworms (nematodes) and tapeworms (cestodes). Nematodes are of two broad types – the ascarids, which are readily visible, may be 100-150 mm long and 2-3 mm in diameter; and the much finer threadworms or *Capillaria*. These, as their name suggests, are like fine cotton threads. The treatment of these parasites has been well covered elsewhere in this book, but it is worth repeating that regular treatment (usually at six-monthly intervals) is essential, and that individual dosing is far more reliable and effective than blanket water medication.

Currently effective treatments are fenbendazole (Panacur® – Hoechst) as mentioned, but there have been a few reports of sudden

121

death in some species with the single large dose technique, or of feather abnormalities developing after the low daily dose course. Levamisole is also effective, but appears to be more bitter tasting.

Tapeworms are occasionally encountered, and can be difficult to diagnose, unless segments are passed in the droppings, appearing as rice-grain-like objects. Birds will be generally unthrifty, and sometimes have chronic diarrhoea. The treatment of choice is praziquantel (Droncit®) which can be given either by injection, or as a crushed tablet, at the same dose rate as recommended for dogs.

BLOOD PARASITES

Many birds harbour protozoan parasites in their blood streams, and most of these appear to be non-pathogenic. There is still considerable research needed on the identification and life-cycles of these parasites, before we can fully understand their clinical significance.

Those that are recognised are perhaps more common in the USA than the UK. *Lankesterella* is one such parasite that is commonly found in passerines such as canaries, and may sometimes be found in cockatiels where red mites are present. The latter act as the vector for the protozoan, which then parasitises the lymphocytes and monocytes in the blood and haemopoietic system. Detection can be difficult on peripheral blood smears, and organisms are more easily found post mortem from impression smears of spleen or bone marrow.

Recent work suggests that the forms of *Lankesterella* visible in the blood are just a part of a life cycle with other stages occurring in the gut, and this species may be involved in the syndrome of 'going light' in many birds.

DISEASES OF THE REPRODUCTIVE SYSTEM

Male birds are rarely affected by such diseases, but hens can suffer from a number of serious conditions.

During the breeding season the body of the hen undergoes considerable changes as a result of hormonal influences in order to produce her clutch of eggs. The ovary becomes considerably enlarged from its quiescent state to produce follicles which release the ova. These pass down the developed oviduct, and during the journey are coated with various layers of albumen, shell membranes, and egg-shell to produce the finished egg. The tubular oviduct becomes very enlarged and vascular, and there is a risk that it may be ruptured, or that the ovum may not be properly collected into the tube. This will result in an accumulation of high protein egg material in the abdominal cavity. The ensuing irritation, inflammation, and infection is called 'egg peritonitis' and is usually rapidly fatal.

The production of egg-shell requires considerable quantities of

122

calcium, and if the hen's diet is deficient in this mineral, or if for some reason her body reserves cannot be mobilised adequately, she will then show signs of hypocalcaemia. This will manifest itself in thin-shelled eggs, smaller or reduced numbers of eggs, muscle weakness and bone 'softening', and difficulty in egg-laying, which can result in 'egg-binding'.

This problem has also been covered elsewhere, and can be caused by oversized or malformed eggs; or by oviduct infection; but it is usually the result of calcium deficiency resulting in reduced muscle activity in the oviduct. The egg then becomes lodged in the distal oviduct or the cloaca, and the bird rapidly weakens, becoming shocked and toxic. In addition to nursing care such as lubrication, increased heat and humidity, and the adminstration of fluids as described, intramuscular calcium (with or without oxytocin) can often produce a rapid delivery, provided there is no physical obstruction, or prolapse of the oviduct.

Simple administration of calcium will not by itself correct a deficiency, as the body's utilisation of this mineral depends on the proper balance of calcium with phosphorus, and also the presence of vitamin D_3 (see Chapter 8).

SEXING
Most of the colour forms of the cockatiel are sexually dimorphic – that is to say that cock and hen are visually differentiated, at least when in adult plumage. The sex can also be determined when the cock bird begins to sing. Some of the newer lighter colour mutations, however, can be more difficult to determine. The plucking of juvenile feathers to hasten the growth of adult plumage may be useful, but in some cases the technique of 'surgical sexing' may be employed.

This procedure has long been used in many species of monomorphic birds, where the sexes are always externally indistinguishable. The gonads of a bird are internal, located at the anterior end of the kidneys, and can be examined with a fibre-optic light source. The technique is well described in many avian publications, and usually requires a general anaesthetic, although some workers use only local anaesthesia. A trocar and cannula is passed through the left flank in the triangular space made by the last rib, the anterior muscle of the thigh, and the sternum, going through both skin and muscle layers. The trocar is then withdrawn, and the fibre-optic illuminated speculum is passed through the cannula. The magnified image of the internal anatomy allows easy inspection of the gonads. Male birds have paired, smooth, oval testes lying between the adrenal gland and the anterior pole of the kidneys. These vary in size according to the age of the bird and phase of the breeding cycle, but are usually pale cream to salmon pink in colour.

The ovary in the cockatiel, in common with that of most bird species, is single, as only the left gonad develops (hence the operation is performed through the left flank). It is a more irregularly shaped organ than the testis, and is usually white to pale grey, with follicles imparting a caviar-like texture. The size of the follicles will vary considerably according to the phase of the breeding cycle.

This method has the advantage over the other sexing techniques of being immediate, and also giving a precise picture of the health and activity of the gonads; it is also at the time of writing far less expensive than other methods. Faecal steroid analysis is unreliable, and chromosome testing is very accurate, but can take at least a week to perform. On the other hand, both these tests are non-invasive and therefore of no risk to the bird.

DEFICIENCY DISEASES

Certain deficiencies in feeding can be a problem in cockatiels. Total nutritional deficiency – i.e. starvation – can be the result of ignorance or neglect on the part of the owner, or of difficulties experienced by the bird in taking food, for example with a damaged beak. In an aviary situation, a weaker bird may be prevented from feeding by its more dominant companions.

A deficiency of some of the lesser minerals and B-vitamins may cause problems, but this is rarely seen in individuals except in experimental conditions as most diets are adequate in these components.

Calcium deficiency is common, either as a result of excessive demand during egg-laying or because of low intake. A bird eating a high seed diet will receive very little calcium, and the oil contained in the seed can in some cases reduce even further the bio-availability of that calcium by binding with it to form insoluble soaps.

Vitamin D deficiency will result in rickets, a bowing deformity of the long bones of the legs, as a consequence of the bones' failure to mineralise properly at their growing ends. Vitamin D is closely linked with calcium metabolism, and the administration of both D_3 and calcium will prevent or treat rickets in the early stages, but if the bones are severely bowed the deformity is irreversible.

Vitamin A deficiency also occurs commonly, especially in birds fed a diet high in sunflower seed. As mentioned earlier, this vitamin is needed for the normal growth and integrity of epithelium, and its lack results in an excessive keratinisation and overgrowth of such tissues, with increased susceptibility to infection. Thick caseous plaques of yellow skin debris may be found in such areas as mouth and throat, and the bird is more likely to have such problems as conjunctivitis and candidiasis.

Vitamin C is not an essential element of the diet, as the cockatiel, in common with many other animal species, is able to manufacture its own.

DRUGS AND DOSAGES

There is little virtue in listing recommended drugs and their dose rates as such a list would be out of date even before it was printed. The pet-bird market is not of great interest to commercial drug companies, so very few medications are produced specifically for cage and aviary birds. This is in marked contrast to the large market for commercially important flocks such as poultry, game birds and pigeons. Most drugs in common usage for cockatiels and other pet birds, therefore, are those produced originally for use in flock birds, dogs and cats, or even humans, which by trial and error in the hands of interested veterinary surgeons and aviculturists have proved useful and efficient.

The range of such drugs is expanding rapidly, as interest in avian medicine develops, and new products are continually being described as effective for birds. Lists of the more commonly used drugs are readily available in existing publications on avian medicine: one particularly useful volume in the UK is *Avian Medicine and Surgery* by Brian Coles. The serious practitioner is recommended to keep up to date with rapid advances by reading journals and periodicals relating to avian treatment.

A few general comments are worth noting: prolonged antibiotic therapy, especially with broad-spectrum drugs, can seriously affect the normal flora of the gut, so an intermittent treatment regime should be used. Alternatively, replacement therapy with natural yogurt, or products such as Transvite® or Can-addase® may be considered.

Preparations of tetracyclines are not well absorbed from the gut in the presence of calcium ions, so the administration of calcium supplements simultaneously with these antibiotics is counterproductive.

Injectable treatment of sick birds is of great value, but it is worth remembering that the injection of a volume as small as 0.1ml into a cockatiel weighing perhaps 100gm is equivalent to giving 25ml to a 25kg dog. Therefore administration must be careful, especially when the bird is debilitated and the muscle mass available is much reduced.

It is hoped that this chapter has given some insight into the disease problems of cockatiels, and that enthusiasts may be pointed in the right direction for nursing and treatment techniques, should their birds begin to show signs of illness or distress.

12 Genetics: An Introduction to Breeding for Colour Mutations

The goal of many enthusiasts is to be able to predict with reasonable accuracy the results of mating normal coloured birds with mutations, or crossing mutations with mutations. The object of this chapter is to endeavour to make the understanding of cockatiel genetics more simple for the majority of keepers and breeders of these birds. For those who wish to fully understand all aspects of genetics, and to treat it as a biological subject, however, a much deeper and broader study should be made.

At the end of the chapter there is a glossary with explanations of the terms used in genetics. To those unfamiliar with the subject many strange-sounding words may be found: These are included for general information. Most, however, will not be included in this particular presentation, as it is considered that although lengthening the text, simple explanations will give better understanding to the learner.

MODE OF INHERITANCE FOR SEX

'Genes' are the germ cells which will evolve to define the characteristics of living things. They are carried on string-like bodies called 'chromosomes' which *act in pairs*. There are many of these present, carrying different signals to form the whole physical make-up. For this section we shall only be concerned with those that carry the instructions for sex, and also happen to carry genes which are responsible for producing some of the colours.

These sex chromosomes are usually defined as X and Y.

X is the male chromosome and the cock has two, so the sex of a cock is designated as XX.

Y is the female sex chromosome. The hen has only one of these, but in addition receives an X chromosome from the cock, so the sex of a hen is designated as XY.

Note: this is exactly opposite to mammals where males are XY and females XX.

At this point one could question: is not XY half cock and half hen? For the purpose of this chapter it will be assumed that X is recessive and Y is dominant, so overcoming the X to produce the female character.

At fertilisation, when the sperm cell from the cock unites with an egg cell from the hen in the upper part of the oviduct, the chromosomes of both cock and hen separate. One X chromosome from the cock unites with one X from the hen to produce a male XX. Alternatively one X from the cock uniting with a Y from the hen produces a female XY.

This separation of the chromosomes ensures that a proportion of both cocks and hens are bred over a period of time. This evolution is known as *sex-linking*.

For the purpose of working out expectations of various matings that will follow, it is essential that this sex-linking be clearly understood when set out as a diagram. In our first diagram each chromosome will be numbered to show how they have paired.

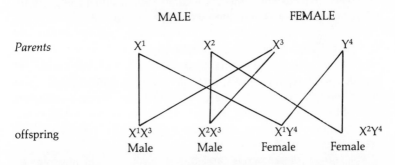

Now the diagram is put into a different form, without the numbers. In this new form the same results are easily ascertained, and allow for simplicity when we come to considering mutations.

	MALES	FEMALES
Parents	XX	XY
Offspring	XX	XY
	XX	XY

This shows that the mating will produce 50 per cent cocks and 50 per cent hens whereas we know in practice that the amount of cocks and hens in a nest will vary; but, as has already been stated, this mode of inheritance assures that over a number of nests both cocks and hens will be bred.

In these diagrams and others that follow, *males are always shown on the left hand side and females on the right*. It is important that the diagram is fully understood. Re-read and set out the diagram yourself to enable ease of understanding for the next sections.

127

MODES OF INHERITANCE FOR COLOUR

There are three different pairs of genes which control colour, and are carried on the chromosomes. The first is in the sex-chromosomes which, as we have already seen, define the sex. This will be known as *Sex-linked*.

The second pair, found in different chromosomes (Autosomes), which have no interaction with the Sex-linked, is referred to as Autosomal-Recessive. For simplicity this will be called *Recessive*.

The third separate set of genes establishing colour is known as *Dominant* as it visually overrides both normal, and all other colours.

This 'Dominant' inheritance has only been found in a Silver mutation, being the first to arise in cockatiels, and is a completely different strain from the earlier Recessive Silvers. It was proven by selective breeding programmes and confirmed in 1986. As this discovery extends the genetic formula needed when mating with other mutations, it is described separately on pp.143.

a) SEX-LINKED COLOUR INHERITANCE

Let us first consider the normal bird, grey in colour. We know that the cock is XX and the hen XY, and that colour is also carried on these chromosomes. For a cock to be grey he must have the grey colour on each of his X chromosomes. If this normal grey colour is designated with a capital letter N in the superscript position, he must be $X^N X^N$ to produce his normal colour.

The colour for the hen is carried on her single X chromosome so she will be $X^N Y$. Her Y chromosome carries no colour and only designates her sex.

At times something happens to one of these normal X^N chromosomes; it becomes altered in its evolution, or *mutates*. From this phenomenon a gene carrying a different colour from normal can arise. From the sex-linked inheritance these colours are

1) Cinnamon
2) Lutino (a bird of white appearance)
3) Pearl

These colours designated with capital letters, again in the superscript position, can replace one normal X^N chromosome and be shown as follows

X^C for Cinnamon
X^L for Lutino
X^P for Pearl

A cock that has mutated would have one X^N chromosome and one X^C, X^L or X^P. However the cock will be normal in appearance as the normal colour is *Dominant* and X^N overrides colours carried on the second chromosome. This second chromosome is known as recessive to normal.

It must be remembered that for a colour to be visual it must be carried on both a cock's X chromosomes. When a cock carries one X^N chromosome with the second defining a colour, he is known as a *split*.

Let us now set out a diagram for mating a cock split for Lutino, with a normal hen. The diagram works exactly as before, but now the colours have been added

	COCK (SPLIT)	HEN (NORMAL)
Parents	$X^N X^L$	$X^N Y$
Offspring	$X^N X^N$	$X^N Y$
	$X^L X^N$	$X^L Y$

Half the cocks with an N on both chromosomes must be normal; the other half with one each colour showing must look normal, but will be split for Lutino. Half the hens will be normal and half Lutino. Remember the hen carries colour on her single X chromosome, and it is for this reason that *hens cannot be split for a sex-linked mutation.*

To obtain Lutino cocks a normal split for Lutino would have to be mated to a Lutino hen.

COCK (SPLIT)	HEN (LUTINO)
$X^L X^N$	$X^L Y$
$X^L X^L$	$X^L Y$
$X^N X^L$	$X^N Y$

Half the cocks are Lutino and half normal split for Lutino. Half the hens will be Lutino and half normal. However, it is important to remember that these are average expectations, and it is most likely that there will be a different mix of cocks and hens in any one nest.

It is hoped that the diagrams are now understood, and that as required, similar programmes can be set out for Cinnamon and Pearl, the other Sex-linked mutations.

Lacewings have not been mentioned: this is because they are genetically the same as Pearl. Lacewing is a term used to describe a feather pattern in different form to the usual Pearl.

It is most vital to remember *that the same colour must appear on both a cock's X chromosomes for it to be visually that colour,* and *for the hen it has only to appear on her one X chromosome.*

Up to this point we have looked at normal to mutation matings, and the next step will be to consider mating mutation to mutation. The diagram for a Cinnamon cock mated to a Lutino hen, is as follows:

CINNAMON COCK $X^C X^C$	LUTINO HEN $X^L Y$
$X^C X^L$	$X^C Y$
$X^C X^L$	$X^C Y$

The hens are clearly Cinnamon. But what are the cocks? With each X a different colour they cannot be visual in either colour. Without two X chromosomes in the same colour in order to overcome normal, normal is the colour that will be seen. Other colours will be present unseen. So the cock will be normal in appearance, but is *double split* for Cinnamon and Lutino.

Let us now mate the double-split cock to a Cinnamon hen.

$X^C X^L$	$X^C Y$
$X^C X^C$	$X^C Y$
$X^L X^C$	$X^L Y$

An interesting combination now appears with two of the Sex-linked mutations being visible. Half the cocks will be Cinnamon, the other half will appear to be normal but are *double-splits* for Lutino and Cinnamon. Half the hens will be Cinnamon and half Lutino.

Let us now set out a diagram involving all three of the Sex-linked mutations. A cock double-split for Lutino and Pearl mated to a Cinnamon hen.

$X^L X^P$	$X^C Y$
$X^L X^C$	$X^L Y$
$X^P X^C$	$X^P Y$

All the cocks will appear normal in colour but half will be double-split for Lutino and Cinnamon and half double-split for Pearl and Cinnamon. Half the hens will be Lutino and half Pearl.

To finalise this section on Sex-linked colour inheritance, we must look at what happens when occasionally there is an interaction of the genes carrying the colours. This takes place before fertilisation and is known as *crossover*.

Crossover

130   The interaction known as crossover does not occur very often, but let us see what can happen to the genes of a cock, normal in

appearance but split for Cinnamon and Pearl. We know that he is designated X^CX^P. The genes on these chromosomes transfer, the ^{P} joins the ^{C}, and we now have $X^{CP}X$. The X without a superscript letter for colour must stand for normal X^N. So $X^{CP}X^N$ is still a normal looking bird but now split for Cinnamon-Pearl, not for Cinnamon and Pearl (Cinnamon/Pearl) as before.

To see the difference in breeding results let us set out diagrams for these two cocks, both paired to a Cinnamon hen.

1

SPLIT FOR CINNAMON AND PEARL X^CX^P	CINNAMON X^CY
X^CX^C X^PX^C	X^CY X^PY

Half the cocks are Cinnamon, half normal double-split for Pearl and Cinnamon. Half the hens are Cinnamon and half Pearl.

2

SPLIT FOR CINNAMON-PEARL $X^{CP}X^N$	CINNAMON X^CY
$X^{CP}X^C$ X^NX^C	$X^{CP}Y$ X^NY

Half the cocks are Cinnamon split for Cinnamon-Pearl and half normal split for Cinnamon. Half the hens are Cinnamon-Pearl and half normal.

This example of crossover has produced quite different results, but from it has arisen a double mutation, a Cinnamon-Pearl hen. Similar effects can occur with the Lutino mutation. As there is no difference in visual appearance when crossover takes place, it is not until the breeding results prove different to what was anticipated, that one can judge what has occurred.

Reverse crossover can also occur in the same manner as crossover: $X^{CP}X^N$ can recrossover back to X^CX^P.

b) RECESSIVE COLOUR INHERITANCE
Recessive colour chromosomes are completely different chromosomes from the sex-linked ones. These are Autosomes which we call *Recessive* for simplicity and because they are recessive to the Dominant normal cockatiel colour.

Each bird has a pair of these chromosomes and a major fact to remember is that *they never pair with the Sex-linked chromosomes.*

Cocks and hens are not considered separately as with 'Recessive' birds the colours are equally inherited, so that mention of sex at this stage is irrelevant.

131

The basic Recessive colours are

1) Fallow
2) Pied
3) Silver
4) White faced

Using a capital N to describe a Normal bird, as its colour will be dominant, and small letters for the others, as they are recessive to normal, we can designate as follows:

Normal	NN
Fallow	ff
Pied	pp
Silver	ss
White faced	ww

As each of the above birds carries an identical pair of colour chromosomes, they will not be split, and their visual colours will be as stated.

Although these chromosomes must be in pairs, one has to be given from each parent. So if a Normal NN is mated to a Pied pp the young, having received one from each parent, will all be Np, that is, half Normal and half Pied, but we must remember that Normal N dominates and masks other colours so that all these young will be normal in colour. These birds will therefore be Normals split for Pied, i.e. Normal/Pied.

As the colours or mix of colours applies equally to cocks and hens, both sexes can be split with the Recessive inheritance.

To show how the chromosomes pair, let us look at a diagram of the results of mating a normal with a pied bird. Initially, to facilitate understanding, a number is appended to each chromosome.

NORMAL	PIED
N1N2	p1p2

N1 p1
N1 p2
N2 p1
N2 p2

132 All the progeny will be normal in colour, split for Pied; that is, Normal/Pied.

When cockatiels are split for Pied they can very often be identified by white feathers on the head or neck or by patches in the normal grey colour. Beware of birds of this appearance being offered as Pieds.

Cockatiels split for any mutation other than Pied do not display these signs.

Let us try mating a Normal/Pied to a Pied, now omitting the numbers.

Np	pp
Np	
Np	
pp	
pp	

Half the birds are Normal/Pied and the other half are Pied.

Let us reiterate that *this is nothing to do with cocks and hens.* It is the average expectation of colours from a nest when mating two Recessive birds. It is also important to remember that this average could take place over a large number of nests; and it could easily happen that all splits could appear in any one nest.

Fallow, Silver or White faced can be similarly diagrammed; so let us mate two Normals split for White faced.

Nw	Nw
NN	
Nw	
wN	
ww	

This gives us 25 per cent Normals, 50 per cent Normals/White faced, and 25 per cent White faced.

To complete this chapter let us consider the sexing symbols for these Recessive mutations.

We know that cocks are XX and hens XY, and also that colours are carried on the X chromosomes for *Sex-linked birds only.* So for Recessive birds the sex-linked chromosomes must be normal $X^N X^N$ for the Cock, $X^N Y$ for the hen.

c) DESIGNATION OF THE COMPLETE MAKE-UP SHOWING BOTH RECESSIVE AND SEX-LINKED SYMBOLS

Recessive

To complete the designation from the last section the Recessive symbols must now be prefaced by the Sex-linked symbols.

	COCKS	HENS
Normal	$X^N X^N$-NN	X^NY-NN
Fallow	$X^N X^N$-ff	X^NY-ff
Pied	$X^N X^N$-pp	X^NY-pp
Silver	$X^N X^N$-ss	X^NY-ss
White faced	$X^N X^N$-ww	X^NY-ww

Splits will be set out in the same way so that a Normal hen split for Pied will be X^NY Np.

Sex-Linked
To finalise we have to consider what the other Recessive genes are signalling and, remembering that as none of these sex-linked colours comes from these Recessive genes, they must all be Normal NN. So we have:

	COCKS	HENS
Cinnamon	$X^C X^C$-NN	X^CY-NN
Lutino	$X^L X^L$-NN	X^LY-NN
Pearl	$X^P X^P$-NN	X^PY-NN

Colour Inheritance from the Mating of Sex-Linked and Recessive Mutations
We now come to the multi-mutations, matings from which were bred some of the most popular and sought-after colours, including the Pearl-Pieds, Cinnamon-Pearl-Pieds, and Albinos (Lutino-White faced).

As an exercise, let us proceed with a programme for breeding Pearl-Pieds, and start with mating a Pearl cock to a Pied hen.

Firstly let us look at their recessive genes

PEARL COCK	PIED HEN
NN	pp

Np
Np
Np
Np

The important point now is that there are four Recessive signals to each of the Sex-linked genes, so that dependant on the mating there could be sixteen results.

A diagram set out with the full genetic make-up of these birds will be

PEARL COCK	PIED HEN
X^PX^P-NN	X^NY-pp
X^PX^N-Np	X^PY-Np
X^PX^N-Np	X^PY-Np
X^PX^N-Np	X^PY-Np
X^PX^N-Np	X^PY-Np
X^PX^N-Np	X^PY-Np
X^PX^N-Np	X^PY-Np
X^PX^N-Np	X^PY-Np
X^PX^N-Np	X^PY-Np

All cocks will be normal split for Pearl and Pied. Remember colour must be shown on both of a pair of chromosomes to overcome normal. In this instance both sexes are split, so all the hens will be Pearl split for Pied. Remember colour is inherited in a hen from a signal on her single Sex-linked chromosome; her Recessive chromosomes are as the cock's, Normal split Pied, so both will carry a hidden Pied mutation.

The next stage will be to mate a cock that is normal split for Pearl and Pied to a hen that is Pearl split for Pied.

COCK NORMAL/PEARL/PIED	HEN PEARL SPLIT PIED
X^PX^N-Np	X^PY-Np
X^PX^P-NN	X^PY-NN
X^PX^P-Np	X^PY-Np
X^PX^P-pN	X^PY-pN
X^PX^P-pp	X^PY-pp
X^NX^P-NN	X^NY-NN
X^NX^P-Np	X^NY-Np
X^NX^P-pN	X^NY-pN
X^NX^P-pp	X^NY-pp

Let us look at the cocks: the first is Pearl, the second and third are Pearl but split for Pied. The fourth must be Pearl-Pied, as colours are signalled on both pairs of genes. The fifth is normal split for Pearl, the sixth and seventh will both be normal split for Pearl and Pied. The eighth must be Pied as his recessive genes are identical, which will overcome normal, but he will be split for Pearl.

The pattern of the hens is slightly different: the fifth will be normal as it is not split on either pair of genes, and the eighth is a pied.

Both a cock and hen Pearl-Pied are shown but as the chance is one in eight, it is not likely to occur in one nest.

A range of the symbols covering various mutations is set out on page 137. The list by no means encompasses all the possibilities, but with reference to the preceding chapters, it should be clear how the symbols have been allocated to show the mutations involved.

By setting out tables, breeders should now be able to assess the probable outcome of matings they wish to consider.

NEW MUTATIONS

Mutations can occur through inbreeding, but more often it is by accident; the genes somehow alter. This can be seen in the wild, where white feathers or wings on blackbirds and sparrows are commonly seen. If a new colour appears in a cockatiel it is at first exciting, but problems immediately become apparent. Firstly the breeder must establish whether it is in fact a genetic mutation, and not a freak caused by some lack of vitamin, or some substance in the feeding. Then it must be preserved and bred to produce a strain. Consideration may be given to breeding from father to daughter, or mother to son, but it would be better to leave the parents together, hoping that more offspring of the new mutation would be produced.

The alternative would be to mate the new mutation to a strong, proven, fertile bird. Whether pure breeds or splits appear, they must be bred back with a very carefully planned programme, using pure-bred, splits and normals to establish a healthy strain, as unfortunately when mutation occurs it can affect other parts of the anatomy. In their early days Lutinos, which have red eyes when young, had poor eyesight, and then more serious problems of eyesight took a heavy toll of the first Silvers. Placings at the show benches in the USA reveal that many of the new mutations are not yet amongst the winners. The problem is of size in Recessive mutations; when ringing their birds, many owners will have noticed the short legs of many of these birds. Breeders are making great efforts, which take a very long time, to breed some of the most beautiful birds up to the physical standard of the normal bird.

Expert advice is recommended before embarking on a breeding programme, and a major point to consider is the large number of aviaries that will be needed (dare a split be parted with!), and the long time span involved. Thirty aviaries and five years could be a conservative estimate.

SELECTION OF SYMBOLS USED FOR PLOTTING DIAGRAMS TO ASSESS MATING RESULTS

COCKS	HENS	MUTATION
$X^N X^L NN$	Cocks only	Normal split for Lutino
$X^N X^N Np$	Cocks only	Normal split for Pied
$X^N X^P Np$	Cocks only	Normal split for Pearl and Pied
$X^P X^P NN$	$X^P Y\ NN$	Pearl
$X^L X^L NN$	$X^L Y\ NN$	Lutino
$X^C X^C NN$	$X^C Y\ NN$	Cinnamon
$X^{CP} X^{CP} NN$	$X^{CP} Y\ NN$	Cinnamon-Pearl
$X^C X^C pp$	$X^C Y\ pp$	Cinnamon-Pied
$X^{CP} X^{CP} pp$	$X^{CP} Y\ pp$	Cinnamon-Pearl-Pied
$X^P X^P pp$	$X^P Ypp$	Pearl-Pied
$X^{LP} X^{LP} NN$	$X^{LP} Y\ NN$	Lutino-Pearl
$X^{LP} X^{LP} pp$	$X^{LP} Y\ pp$	Lutino-Pearl-Pied
$X^N X^N ff$	$X^N Y\ ff$	Fallow
$X^N X^N pp$	$X^N Y\ pp$	Pied
$X^N X^N ss$	$X^N Y\ ss$	Silver
$X^N X^N ww$	$X^N Y\ ww$	White faced
$X^P X^P Np$	$X^P Y\ Np$	Pearl split for Pied
$X^N X^P pp$	Cocks only	Pied split for Pearl
$X^P X^{CP} pp$	Cocks only	Pearl-Pied split for Cinnamon
$X^P X^{CLP} pp$	Cocks only	Pearl-Pied split for Cinnamon Lutino
$X^C X^{CLP} pp$	Cocks only	Cinnamon-Pied split for Lutino Pearl
Hens only	$X^C Y\ pw$	Cinnamon split for Pied and White faced
Hens only	$X^N Y\ pw$	Normal split for Pied and White faced

SCHEDULES OF BREEDING EXPECTATIONS

For easy reference these are set out showing colour expectations from various matings, and the sexes of the offspring where possible. The schedules do not cover all matings, as there are over one hundred possible combinations from the mutations, and when splits and crossovers are taken into consideration, the number rises to over two thousand.

CINNAMON PAIRING COMBINATIONS

COCK	HEN	OFFSPRING
Normal	Cinnamon	All cocks Normal/Cinnamon All hens Normal
Cinnamon	Normal	All cocks Normal/Cinnamon All hens Cinnamon

COCK	HEN	OFFSPRING
Normal/ Cinnamon	Cinnamon	Half the cocks Cinnamon and half Normal/Cinnamon Half the hens Cinnamon and half Normal
Cinnamon	Lutino	All cocks Normal/Cinnamon/Lutino All hens Cinnamon
Lutino	Cinnamon	All cocks Normal/Lutino/Cinnamon All hens Lutino
Cinnamon	Pearl	All cocks Normal/Cinnamon/Pearl All hens Cinnamon
Pearl	Cinnamon	All cocks Normal/Pearl/Cinnamon All hens Pearl
Cinnamon	Pied	All cocks Normal/Cinnamon/Pied All hens Cinnamon/Pied
Pied	Cinnamon	All cocks Normal/Pied/Cinnamon All hens Normal/Pied
Normal/ Cinnamon/ Pearl	Cinnamon	Cocks half Cinnamon half Normal/Pearl/Cinnamon Half hens Cinnamon half Pearl
Note: If crossover took place on this mating, the results would be:		Half the cocks Cinnamon/Pearl half Normal/Cinnamon Half the hens Cinnamon-Pearl and half Normal
Cinnamon-Pearl	Cinnamon-Pied	All cocks Cinnamon/Pearl/Pied All hens Cinnamon-Pearl/Pied
Cinnamon-Pearl	Pearl-Pied	Half the cocks Pearl/Pied and half Cinnamon/Pied Half the hens Pearl/Pied and half Cinnamon/Pied
Pearl-Pied	Cinnamon-Pearl	All cocks Pearl/Cinnamon/Pied All hens Pearl/Pied
Cinnamon-Pearl/Pied	Cinnamon-Pearl-Pied	Half the cocks Cinnamon-Pearl-Pied and half Cinnamon-Pearl/Pied Half the hens Cinnamon-Pearl-Pied and half Cinnamon-Pearl/Pied
Cinnamon-Pied	Pied	All cocks Pied/Cinnamon All hens Cinnamon-Pied

COCK	HEN	OFFSPRING
Cinnamon-Pied/Pearl	Cinnamon-Pearl-Pied	Half the cocks Cinnamon-Pearl-Pied and half Cinnamon-Pied/Pearl Half the hens Cinnamon-Pearl-Pied and half Cinnamon-Pied
Cinnamon-Pearl-Pied	Pearl-Pied	All cocks Pied/Cinnamon/Pearl All hens Cinnamon-Pearl-Pied

LUTINO PAIRINGS

COCK	HEN	OFFSPRING
Lutino	Normal	All cocks Normal/Lutino All hens Lutino
Normal	Lutino	All cocks Normal/Lutino All hens Normal
Lutino	Pearl	All cocks Normal/Lutino/Pearl All hens Lutino
Pearl	Lutino	All cocks Normal/Pearl/Lutino All hens Pearl
Lutino	Cinnamon	All cocks Normal/Lutino/Cinnamon All hens Lutino
Normal/ Lutino/Pearl	Lutino	Half the cocks Lutino and half Normal/Pearl/Lutino Half the hens Lutino and half Pearl
Note: If crossover* took place on this mating the results would be		Half the cocks Lutino/Pearl and half Normal/Lutino Half the hens Lutino-Pearl and half Normal
Lutino	Lutino-Pearl	All cocks Lutino/Pearl All hens Lutino
Lutino-Pearl	Lutino	All cocks Lutino/Pearl All hens Lutino-Pearl

*It is from this crossover of the genes that Lutino-Pearl would be bred. This cannot be controlled; it just happens from time to time.

PEARL PAIRINGS

COCK	HEN	OFFSPRING
Pearl	Normal	All cocks Normal/Pearl All hens Pearl
Normal	Pearl	All cocks Normal/Pearl All hens Normal
Pearl	Cinnamon	All cocks Normal/Pearl/Cinnamon All hens Pearl
Cinnamon	Pearl	All cocks Normal/Cinnamon/Pearl All hens Cinnamon
Pearl	Pied	All cocks Normal/Pearl/Pied All hens Pearl/Pied
Pied	Pearl	All cocks Normal/Pearl/Pied All hens Normal/Pied
Pearl-Pied	Pied	All cocks Pied/Pearl All hens Pearl-Pied
Pied	Pearl-Pied	All cocks Pied/Pearl All hens Pied
Cinnamon-Pearl	Pearl-Pied	All cocks Pearl/Cinnamon/Pied All hens Cinnamon-Pearl/Pied
Pearl/ Cinnamon/ Pied	Pearl-Pied	Cocks 25% Pearl-Pied Cocks 25% Pearl-Pied/Cinnamon Cocks 25% Pearl/Pied Cocks 25% Pearl/Cinnamon/Pied Hens 25% Pearl-Pied Hens 25% Pearl/Pied Hens 25% Cinnamon-Pearl/Pied Hens 25% Cinnamon-Pearl-Pied

FALLOW PAIRINGS

COCK	HEN	OFFSPRING
Fallow	Lutino	All cocks Normal/Lutino/Fallow All hens Normal/Fallow
Lutino	Fallow	All cocks Normal/Lutino/Fallow All hens Lutino/Fallow

COCK	HEN	OFFSPRING
Fallow Pied	Pied } Fallow }	All cocks and hens Normal/Fallow/Pied
Fallow	Pearl	All cocks Normal/Pearl/Fallow All hens Normal/Fallow
Pearl	Fallow	All cocks Normal/Pearl/Fallow All hens Pearl/Fallow

PIED PAIRINGS

COCK	HEN	OFFSPRING
Pied	Normal	All cocks and hens Normal/Pied
Normal	Pied	All cocks and hens Normal/Pied
Pied	Pearl	All cocks Normal/Pearl/Pied All hens Normal/Pied
Pearl	Pied	All cocks Normal/Pearl/Pied All hens Pearl/Pied
Pied	Cinnamon	All cocks Normal/Pied/Cinnamon All hens Normal/Pied
Cinnamon	Pied	All cocks Normal/Cinnamon/Pied All hens Cinnamon/Pied
Pied	Lutino	All cocks Normal/Lutino/Pied All hens Normal/Pied
Lutino	Pied	All cocks Normal/Lutino/Pied All hens Lutino/Pied
Cinnamon- Pearl-Pied	Pearl	All cocks Pearl/Cinnamon/Pied All hens Cinnamon-Pearl/Pied
Cinnamon- Pearl-Pied	Pearl-Pied	All cocks Pearl-Pied/Cinnamon All hens Cinnamon-Pearl-Pied
Cinnamon- Pearl/Pied	Cinnamon- Pearl-Pied	Half the cocks Cinnamon-Pearl-Pied and half Pearl-Pied/Cinnamon Half the hens Cinnamon-Pearl-Pied and half Pearl-Pied
Pearl-Pied	Cinnamon- Pearl-Pied	All cocks Pearl-Pied/Cinnamon All hens Pearl-Pied

COCK	HEN	OFFSPRING
Cinnamon-Pied/Pearl	Cinnamon-Pearl-Pied	Half cocks Cinnamon-Pearl-Pied and half Cinnamon-Pied/Pearl Half the hens Cinnamon-Pearl-Pied and half Cinnamon-Pied

SILVER RECESSIVE PAIRINGS

COCK	HEN	OFFSPRING
Silver	Normal	All cocks and hens Normal/Silver
Normal	Silver	All cocks and hens Normal/Silver
Silver	Pearl	All cocks Normal/Pearl/Silver All hens Normal/Silver
Pearl	Silver	All cocks Normal/Pearl/Silver All hens Pearl/Silver
Silver	Lutino	All cocks Normal/Lutino/Silver All hens Normal/Silver
Lutino	Silver	All cocks Normal/Lutino/Silver All hens Lutino/Silver
Silver	Cinnamon	All cocks Normal/Cinnamon/Silver All hens Normal/Silver
Cinnamon	Silver	All cocks Normal/Cinnamon/Silver All hens Cinnamon/Silver
Silver	Pied	All cocks and hens Normal/Silver/Pied
Pied	Silver	All cocks and hens Normal/Silver/Pied
Normal/Pearl/Silver	Pearl/Silver	The possibilities in cocks and hens are Normal/Pearl, Pearl, Pearl/Silver, Silver-Pearl, Normal/Silver/Pearl, Silver/Pearl and a proportion of Silver hens

WHITE FACED PAIRINGS

COCK	HEN	OFFSPRING
White faced	White faced	Both cocks and hens White faced
White faced	Normal	Both cocks and hens Normal/White faced

COCK	HEN	OFFSPRING
Normal	White faced	Both cocks and hens Normal/White faced
White faced	Lutino	All cocks Normal/Lutino/White faced All hens Normal/White faced
White faced	Pied	Both cocks and hens Normal/White faced/Pied
Pearl	White faced	All cocks Normal/Pearl/white faced All hens Pearl/White faced

DOMINANT SILVER PAIRINGS

This is the first Dominant colour mutation to appear in cockatiels, and as Dominant Silver will override both normal and other colours, the breeding results of combinations with other mutations are different from those of Recessive Silver.

COCK	HEN	OFFSPRING
Silver DF	Normal	Both cocks and hens, Silver SF
Normal	Silver DF	Both cocks and hens, Silver SF
Silver SF	Normal	Half of both cocks and hens Silver SF and half Normal
Pearl	Silver SF	Half the cocks Silver SF/Pearl and half Normal/Pearl Half the hens Silver SF, Pearl and half Pearl
Silver SF	Pied	Half of both cocks and hens Silver SF Pied and half Normal/Pied
Pied	Silver SF	Half of both cocks and hens Silver SF/Pied and half Normal/Pied

THE DOMINANT SILVER MUTATION (OR DILUTE)

The breeding programme to prove this new strain revealed that there was a double and single factor in the colour. With the double factor the colour is further diluted and appears paler.

Previously we have seen the breeding expectations of combining birds of Sex-linked and Recessive inheritance; now we have a third avenue of inheritance, *Dominant*, where a dominant colour that overrides both normal and other colours has to be taken into consideration.

To express this third set of genes, capital letters SS will be used to designate a Dominant Silver, double factor, and only one capital S will be used to designate a Dominant Silver single factor. From the breeding expectations SS double factor is expressed as DF, and SN single factor as SF.

A capital N has previously been used when a colour has not been present, so for continuity this will now apply when the third pair of genes is not active. A normal cock can therefore be described genetically as $X^N X^N$. NN.NN and a hen $X^N Y$.NN.NN.

The Dominant Silver double factor cock will be $X^N X^N$.NN.SS and a single factor cock is $X^N X^N$.NN.SN, with the hens $X^N Y$.NN.SS and $X^N Y$.NN.SN.

We will now consider the expectations of breeding a Dominant Silver DF cock to a Normal hen.

It must firstly be stressed that each set of genes acts separately, and will not mix. The interchange of genes can only take place with its own sort.

Before using diagrams as previously shown, this mating is broken down to show the action of each set of genes separately.

DOMINANT SILVER DF COCK   NORMAL HEN

$X^N X^N$.NN.SS $X^N Y$.NN.NN

The Sex-linked chromosomes produce

COCKS   HENS
$X^N X^N$ $X^N Y$

The Recessive chromosomes produce

NN   NN

The Dominant Silver chromosomes produce

SN   SN

The complete combination is

$X^N X^N$.NN.SN $X^N Y$.NN.SN

With the S overriding other colours the result is the same for both cocks and hens, Silver SF.

Now using the 'T' diagram, pairing the chromosomes exactly as above, let us plot the expectations of mating a Pearl cock to a Silver SF hen.

PEARL COCK	SILVER SF HEN
$X^P X^P$.NN.NN	$X^N Y$.NN.SN
$X^P X^N$.NN.NS	$X^P Y$.NN.NS
NN.NN	NN.NN
$X^P X^N$.NN.NS	$X^P Y$.NN.NS
NN.NN	NN.NN

144

Half the cocks will be Silver SF/Pearl and half Normal/Pearl. Half the hens will be Silver SF/Pearl and half Pearl.

To combine a Dominant Silver with a Recessive mutation let us mate a Silver SF cock to a Pied hen.

COCK	HEN
X^NX^N.NN.SN	X^NY.pp.NN
X^NX^N.Np.SN	X^NY.Np.SN
Np.NN	Np.NN
X^NX^N.Np.SN	X^NY.Np.SN
Np.NN	Np.NN

Half both cocks and hens will be Silver SF/Pied and half Normal/Pied.

Matings with other mutations can be dealt with in the same manner, and as this new Silver mutation becomes freely available many will be tried. Breeders look forward to the appearance of a pure Silver, from combining with the White faced.

GLOSSARY OF TERMS USED IN GENETICS

Alleles Two genes, occupying the same place on the chromosome, and affecting the same character, but in different ways. Each characteristic of an organism is usually determined by a pair of genes called alleles, the genotype thus consists of a number of alleles.

Autosomes Chromosomes which are not involved with sex determination.

Chromosomes String-like bodies which carry the genes.

Dominant A gene which dominates its contrasting allele, the colour of which is visual and suppresses other colours.

Gametes The reproductive egg cells from the hen, and the sperm cells from the cock.

Genes The germ cells situated on the chromosomes, which carry the modes of inheritance, including those of sex and colour.

Genotype The genetic constitution of an organism as determined by its genes. For example, a Pied/Lutino cockatiel is visually Pied, and the Lutino colour is invisible; it is a Pied split Lutino genotype.

145

Heterozygous From Greek, meaning different: contrasting alleles for the same character. Impurely bred cockatiels from the mating of different mutations will produce offspring of different colours, not all visible.

Homozygous From Greek, meaning the same. Identical alleles for a particular characteristic. When pure bred cockatiels of the same colour are mated, the offspring are the same colour as the parents.

Mendel The Austrian monk, Gregor Johann Mendel (1822-84), who studied natural science in Vienna, and devoted his life as an abbot to laying the foundation for the whole theory of heredity.

Phenotype The visible characteristics of an organism. In cockatiels this will designate the visual colour, but not necessarily embrace the total genetic make-up. For example, a Pied split Lutino genotype is a Pied phenotype.

Punnett Square A diagram or grid called after one of the early geneticists, R.C. Punnett, who first used this method to analyse breeding results. We do not find the Punnett square practical for complex matings, where combinations of more than two mutations are involved.

Recessive Refers to a colour gene that is overridden and masked by a Dominant colour gene. Until the advent of the Dominant Silver all cockatiel mutations were recessive to normal.

Zygote The union of an egg cell from the hen, and a sperm cell from the cock; a fertilised egg.

13   Show Standards

Many people like to show their cockatiels, and derive great pleasure from attending shows and meeting other competitors. Others who do not wish to show themselves like to attend shows in order to see the type and standard of birds being shown.

I am extremely grateful to the American Cockatiel Society for their great kindness in allowing the publication of their show standards for cockatiels in this book.

Unfortunately there are no cockatiel show standards at present in the UK, and neither is there a society dedicated only to the interests of cockatiels although no doubt this will alter in years to come.

The Parrot Society of Great Britain, which has some thousands of members in the UK and other countries, caters for all parrot-type birds, but is dedicated to the care and conservation of parrots and parakeets; it does not lay down show standards for any birds.

Likewise the Avicultural Society, an organisation with members all over the world, has been actively promoting the well-being, conservation and breeding of all types of Birds since 1894; but it does not concern itself with the showing of domesticated species such as the cockatiel.

THE AMERICAN COCKATIEL SOCIETY SHOW STANDARD

GENERAL CONFORMATION
The Cockatiel is a long bird, with graceful proportions, but of good substance (full bodied). From the top of the shoulder curve to the tip of the wing, from the top of the skull to the vent, and from the vent to the tip of the tail (ideally) should measure 7 in. The goal being a 14 in bird with a 3in crest. The total bird being 17 in.

Crest
Should be long (goal 3 in), with good density, curving from the top of the cere fanning out to give fullness.

Head
Should be large and well rounded with no flat spot on top or back of the skull. Baldness will be faulted according to the degree of severity of each bird on the show bench. Our aim is for no bald spot even in Lutinos. The eyes should be large, bright and alert, and placed at mid-point between front and back of the skull. The brow should be well pronounced. When viewed from the front, the brow should protrude enough to indicate good breadth between the eyes. The

beak should be clean, of normal length, and tucked in so the lower mandible is partially visible.

Cheek patches should be uniformly rounded, well defined (no bleeding), and brightly coloured (especially on the males). Adult male cockatiels will have a bright, clear, yellow head, sharply defined where the yellow meets the border of the main body feathers. A deep bib is preferred. There should be no evidence of pin feathers.

Neck
Should be relatively long, have a very slight curvature above the shoulders and have a small nip above the chest area, giving the bird a graceful outline and eliminating the appearance of a 'bull' neck or the 'ramrod' posture of some psittacine species. An exaggerated 'snake' neck would be reason for fault.

Body
The body of the cockatiel when viewed strictly from the side angle can be somewhat deceptive, as only a well rounded outline of the chest will indicate whether the specimen has good substance. A frontal (or back) view shows more truly the great breadth through the chest (and shoulder) areas of an adult cockatiel (more prevalent in hens). It is the strong muscular development that enables the cockatiel to be such a strong flier. A cockatiel should have a high, broad, full chest (more prevalent in hens); a slender, tapering abdomen; a wide, straight back (no hump or sway); and be a large, sleek bird.

Wings
Should be large, wide and long, enveloping most of the body from a side view. Should be held tightly to the body, tips close to the tail with no drooping of the shoulders or crossing of the wings. The wing patch should be wide (goal of $\frac{3}{4}$ in at the widest point), well defined and clear of darker feathers. All flight feathers should be in evidence. Covert feathers should illustrate their growth pattern clearly.

Legs and Feet
Should hold the bird erect at approximately 70 degrees off the horizontal. Must grasp the perch firmly (two toes forward and two back), be clean, and claws not overgrown or missing.

Tail
The longest flights should be the extension of an imaginary line straight through the center of the bird's body. A humped back will cause the tail to sag too low, and a 'swayed' back might elevate the tail higher than desired. The feathers themselves should be straight,

148

clean and neither frayed, split or otherwise out of line. All flights should be in evidence.

CONDITION
A bird in top condition has clean, tight feathers: no frayed or missing feathers, no half grown or pin feathers. The beak and claws must be of suitable length. There should be no unnatural roughness or scaling on the cere, beak, legs or feet. If a bird is in good condition, it will be almost impossible to get it wet. Water will roll off like it does off a duck.

DEPORTMENT
In a good show stance, a cockatiel should indicate a central line approximately 70 degrees off the horizontal. It will present and display well on the perch.

CLASSIFICATIONS ON TYPES
The following categories concern specific coloration aspects of the Normal and Mutant cockatiels. While definition is necessary for each type, it is to be remembered that coloration is not as emphasized on the show bench as it may appear to be in the written standard. (See Point Standard.)

Normals
The color should be a dark grey, ideally uniform in color throughout.

Pieds
The ideal Pied will be 75% yellow and 25% dark grey. The goal being yellow pied markings over white pied markings. The aim being for tail and wing flights to be totally clear. The mask area should be clear, with no grey to create a 'dirty' effect. Symmetry of pied markings are ideal.

Lutinos
Ideally a rich, deep buttercup yellow throughout. Long tail feathers and primary flights will not be severely faulted for being a lighter shade of yellow than the body.

Pearl Hens
Extensive 'heavy' pearl markings that are well defined, uniform and without splotching. Ideally the pearl markings will be a deep buttercup yellow.

Pearl Males
The same as for hens with less influence placed on the pearl markings.

149

Cinnamons
The colour should be cinnamon, uniform in color throughout.

Fallows
The color should be light cinnamon with a yellow suffusion, uniform in color throughout. The eyes should be ruby or red.

Silvers
The color should be a dull metallic silver, uniform in color throughout. The eyes should be ruby or red.

White Faced
Same as the Normal void of all lipochrome. The mask area of the cock will be pure white.

Albinos
Will be void of all lipochrome, a pure white bird with ruby or red eyes. Primaries and flight feathers will not be severely faulted for being an off shade of white.

Cross-Mutations
Will be judged by combining the color standards for all mutations involved.

Splits
Markings on split birds will not be penalized, as these represent a genetic factor of birds split to pied and are not a matter of faulty breeding. A bird showing the split mark is split to pied. It can be split to other mutations but will not show the split markings.

A.C.S. SHOW CAGE
Dimensions
17 in high, 18 in wide and 10 in deep.

Front
Chrome, removable roll-top.

Perches
Two $\frac{3}{4}$ in dowels perpendicular to front.

Paint Color
Inside: light blue semi-gloss. Sherwin Williams color 48966X 'dainty blue' or Pittsburg color P2693 'blueberry frost'. Outside: a high gloss black.

150

Feed and Water

An appropriate seed mix will cover the bottom of the cage (not to exceed 1 in in depth). Water containers (tubes or bottles) that can be removed without opening the cage, as they will be removed during judging.

BANDS

Double banded cockatiels will not be permissible at A.C.S. Regional or Specialty Shows. All other shows are governed by the Club having the show. Double banded birds will be considered as untraceable with no band number recorded on the A.C.S. Show Report, consequently no Champion points will be awarded.

Exceptions to double banding are:

(1) States that require a cockatiel to be banded with a state band will not be considered double banded providing they are banded with a traceable band.

(2) The show secretary shall verify the state required band and mark the show report as such. The cage tag will be marked on the front upper left corner 'D.B.' to designate the cockatiel is also banded with a state band.

A.C.S. POINT STANDARD

The A.C.S. Point Standard has been formulated strictly as an aid for reference to both the judge and exhibitor in choosing the best birds. At show time, all birds will be judged by the comparison method, using the point standard as a guide.

Conformation: 60 Points

(1) *Size: 20 points*

Overall length of bird (ideally 14 in) not including the crest.

(2) *Crest: 10 points*

Length and density of equal importance (ideally 3 in).

(3) *Body Substance: 10 points*

Depth & breadth.

(4) *Proportions: 5 points*

Relationship of head size to body, to tail, to wings. (Ideally 7, 7, 7)

(5) *Wing Carriage: 5 points*

No drooping shoulders or crossed wing tips.

(6) *Tail: 5 points*

All feathers grown and in place, clean and unfrayed.

(7) *Head: 5 points*

Large and well rounded. Eyes large, bright and alert. Brow well pronounced. Beak clean, normal length and tucked in. Cheek patches uniformly rounded and brightly coloured. Bib deep.

Condition: 15 Points
Bird in obvious good health, tight feathered and immaculate.

Deportment: 10 Points
Steadiness and posture, basically the result of thorough show training.

Color and Markings: 10 Points
See the A.C.S. Show Standard for details under each type's classification.

(1) *Uniformity of Color: 5 points*
Uniformity in Normals, Lutinos, Cinnamons, Fallows, Silvers, White Face & Albinos. Markings on Pieds, Pearls & Cross Mutations.
(2) *Depth of Color: 5 points*
Depth of color or degree of markings.

Caging: 5 Points
All cockatiels must be shown in A.C.S. standard type show cages when judged by A.C.S. Panel Judges. The cleanliness of these cages and general condition in reference to upkeep will be weighed by the judge.

Bibliography

Arnell, L., and Keymer, Ian F. (1975) *Bird Diseases*, T.F.H.
Publications Inc. Ltd.

Association of Avian Veterinarians, Volume 7 Nos. 1-4, 1986, East
Northport, New York.

Burnett (1986) *Essential Genetics*, Cambridge University Press.

Cole, B. H. (1985) *Avian Medicine and Surgery*, Blackwell Scientific
Publications, Oxford.

Coles, T. G., 'Dilute or Blackeyed Silver Cockatiel', *Magazine of the
Parrot Society, Volume V, No. 10*, (1981).

Cooper, N. D., 'The Whitefaced Cockatiel', *Magazine of the Parrot
Society, Volume XV, No. 9*, (1981).

Cragg, Peter, C.D.V.M. Texas, 'Phosphorus and Vitamin D3 makes
calcium a "good egg"', *National Cockatiel Society*, Journal No. 3,
(June 1986).

Evans, Stewart, and Fidler, Mike *The Gouldian Finch*, 1986, page
64. Blandford Press, Artillery House, Artillery Row, London
SW1P 1RT, England.

Ford, James D., 'Mother's Nature's Conditioning Food' *Journal of
American Federation of Aviculture*, April-May (1982).

Forshaw, Joseph M., (1981) *Parrot of Australia*, Lansdown Editions,
Melbourne, Australia.

Grau, G. R. Department of Avian Sciences, University of
California, Davis, USA. 'Psittacine Research Project of the
Department into Nutrition. Physiology and Management of a
Flock of 230 Cockatiels and 50 Orange Winged Amazon Parrots',
Cage and Aviary Birds (27/4/85).

Hayward, Jim, 'Choosing a Site for your Aviary', *Parrot Breeder*
No. 6, 1985, W. and P. Hayward, The Aviculturist Publications,
Carterton Breeding Aviaries, Brize Norton Road, Carterton,
Oxford, England.

Lendon, Dr Alan H. (1973 and 1976), *Australian Parrots in Field and
Aviary*, Angus and Robertson.

Manual of Exotic Pets, Revised Edition 1985, published by British
Small Animal Veterinary Association, Cheltenham.

Petrak, M. L. (1982) (as Editor), *Diseases of Cage and Aviary Birds*,
Lea & Febiger, Philadelphia.

Smith, G. A., *Encylopedia of Cockatiels* (1978) TFH Incorporated
Ltd.

Smith, G. A., MRCVS 'The First Dominant Cockatiel Mutation',
Cage and Aviary Birds (April 30, 1983).

Squyres, Tom, 'Mutation Numbers V & VI', *Magazine of American*

Cockatiel Society, Volume 10, No. 3, (1986).

Stoodley, John and Pat (1983), *Parrot Production.* Published by Bezels Publications, Lovefean, Portsmouth PO8 0SW, Great Britain.

Stringer, Roy 'Roy Stringer's Tip of the Week' *Cage and Aviary Birds,* (March 1985).

Thompson, Dale R. 'Cockatiel Mutations' *A.F.A. Watchbird,* Vol. 4, Vol. 9 (1982).

Vredenbregt, J. *Cage and Aviary Birds* ('Food Needs of Parakeets and Parrots', November 15, 1986).

Useful Addresses

GREAT BRITAIN

The Avicultural Society, The Secretary, Warren Hill, Halford's Lane, Hartley Wintney, Hampshire RG27 8AG, England. Quarterly Magazine.

Cage and Aviary Birds (Prospect Magazines), Prospect House, 9-13 Ewell Road, Cheam, Surrey SM1 499, England. Phone: 01-661 4491). Weekly Magazine (Worldwide Distribution).

Casella Ltd., Old Street, London.

Dave Axtell, The European Aviculture Council, P.O. Box 74, Bury St Edmunds, Suffolk IP30 OHS, England. (This organisation has been formed to protect the rights of bird keepers in the UK and Europe.)

Gloucester Laboratories (Veterinary) Ltd., St. Oswald's Road, Cattle Market, Gloucester GL1 29J, England. Phone: 0452 24961. Post Mortem Service.

Marsh Turn X and Roll X Incubators, Robin Haigh, Abbey Bridge Farmhouse, Colonel's Lane, Chertsey, Surrey, England. Phone: Chertsey 60236. Incubators.

Ministry of Agriculture, ADAS (Agricultural Development Advisory Services), Epsom Road, Guildford, Surrey, England. Phone: 0483 62881 Ext. 292). (This service would be most helpful to those with a lot of land, who wish to grow some of their own seed crops.)

Ministry of Agriculture and Fisheries, Animal Health Division, Hq. Government Buildings, Hook Rise, Tolworth, Surrey, England. Phone: 01-337 6611. (For Export and Import Licences.)

Ministry of Agriculture and Fisheries, Animal Health Office, Belfast, Northern Ireland. Phone: 0232-650111 Ext. 289. (For Export and Import Licences for Northern Ireland.)

Ministry of Environment, Headquarters Buildings, Tolworth Towers, Surbiton, Surrey, England. Phone 01-399 5191. (For Export and Import Licences.)

N.C.A. National Council for Aviculture, Jack Prior, Secretary, 87
   Winn Road, Lee, London SE12 9EY, England.

Oaklands Park Farm Aviaries, Newdigate, Nr. Dorking, Surrey,
   England. Phone: 029-384-408. Commercial Establishments
   selling birds, aviaries, cages, seeds, accessories and all equipment
   (Paul and June Bailey).

The Parrot Society, The Secretary, 19A De Parys Avenue, Bedford,
   Bedfordshire, England. Phone: 0234 58922. Monthly Magazine.

Southern Aviaries, Brook House Farm, Tinker's Lane, Hadlow
   Down, Nr. Uckfield, East Sussex, England. Phone: 082-585-283
   (Mr Max Sanderson).

WD-40 Company Ltd., PO Box 440, Milton Keynes.

USA
American Cockatiel Society Inc., The Editor, 1801-19th Avenue,
   N.E. MPLS, Minnesota 55418, USA. Bi-monthly magazines.
   Caters for all aspects of Cockatiel Keeping.

or: American Cockatiel Society Inc., Mr and Mrs Tom and Dee Dee
   Squyres, 9812 Bois d'Arc Ct., Fort Worth, Texas 76126, USA.

A.F.A. American Federation of Aviculture, P.O. Box 1568,
   Redondo Beach, California 90278, USA. Bi-Monthly magazines
   dealing with all aspects of Aviculture.

Lyon Electric Co. Inc., San Diego, California, USA.

National Cockatiel Society, 3402 Williams Street, Marietta, Georgia
   30062.

In case of Teflon or Silverstone Poisoning, Phone National Animal
   Poisons Control Center in Illinois (217) 333-3611.

Index

158